Ordnance Survey
North York Moors Walks

Pathfinder Guide

Compiled by Brian Conduit

JARROLD

Key to colour coding

The walks are divided into three broad categories, indicated by the following colours:

Short, easy walks

Walks of moderate length, likely to involve some modest uphill walking

More challenging walks, which may be longer and/or over more rugged terrain, often with some stiff climbs

Acknowledgements

I would like to thank Mr J. R. Goodman and the staff of the National Park Authority for looking at the manuscript and giving me much useful advice.

While every care has been taken to ensure the accuracy of the route directions, the publishers cannot accept responsibility for errors or omissions, or for changes in details given. It has to be emphasised that the countryside is not static: hedges and fences can be removed, field boundaries can alter, footpaths can be rerouted and changes of ownership can result in the closure or diversion of some concessionary paths. Also paths that are easy and pleasant for walking in fine conditions may become slippery, muddy and difficult in wet weather and stepping stones over rivers and streams may become impassable.

Ordnance Survey   ISBN 0-319-00214-4
Jarrold Publishing   ISBN 0-7117-0460-0

First published 1990 by Ordnance Survey and Jarrold Publishing

Ordnance Survey
Romsey Road
Maybush
Southampton SO9 4DH

Jarrold Publishing
Barrack Street
Norwich NR3 1TR

© Crown copyright 1990
Printed in Great Britain by Jarrold Printing, Norwich. 1/90

Previous page: *the magnificent sweep of Robin Hood's Bay from Ravenscar*

Contents

Introduction to the North York Moors

Of all the National Parks, the North York Moors has probably the most clearly defined physical boundaries, making the road signs informing you that you are entering this closely-knit region almost superfluous. On three sides it is buttressed by hills that rise above the surrounding lowlands in a semi-circular arc: on the north the mountain-like Cleveland Hills overlook the Cleveland Plain and valley of the Tees; on the west the abrupt escarpment of the Hambleton Hills looks out over the vales of York and Mowbray to the distant Pennines; and on the south the lower, less sharply defined and more broken Tabular Hills look across the Vale of Pickering to the line of the Yorkshire Wolds. The circle is completed on the east by the most unmistakable frontier of all — the North Sea.

A series of market towns — Guisborough, Stokesley, Northallerton, Thirsk, Helmsley and Pickering — lie near the foot of this moorland massif in a similar semi-circular arc, serving as the gateways into the region. Completing the circle are the major coastal towns of Scarborough and Whitby whose main means of contact with the outside world, at least before the Victorian railway era, was the sea. Within the Moors there are no towns, but as fine a collection of attractive and unspoilt villages and hamlets as one could wish to visit. Many of these comprise a single wide street lined by spacious greens where, as at Hutton-le-Hole and Goathland, the sheep that nibble the grass not only give the greens a well cropped and neat appearance but also bring village and moor together in a harmonious and integral relationship.

Undoubtedly the chief glory of the North York Moors is the heather. Here are the most extensive and continuous heathery expanses in the country, which in late summer and early autumn become a vast and unbroken carpet of pink and purple that makes an unforgettable sight. The moors are wide, wild and open, rising to their highest point at 1490 feet (454m) on Urra Moor; but in the southern part of the National Park they are cut into by a number of dales, running roughly parallel to each other from north to south. The bright green fields, neat farms and drystone walls of these dales contrast vividly with the more sombre brown and purple of the enveloping moors. Each has its individual characteristics: Bilsdale is wide and fertile; lovely Ryedale possesses Rievaulx, that most superlative of monastic ruins; Bransdale is lonely and remote — it is known as Kirk Dale in its lower reaches; Farndale is famed for its spring display of daffodils and Rosedale's sparse population and rural tranquillity make it almost impossible to believe that only a century ago it was the scene of intense iron-mining activity.

A series of high ridges ('riggs') separate these dales, and the narrow streams (most boasting the title river) that water them — the Rye, Hodge Beck, Dove and Seven — flow southwards into the Vale of Pickering and on via the Ouse to the Humber Estuary. Further north where the moorland is less broken is the valley of the Esk, the area's only major river and the only one that flows directly eastwards to the coast. Fed by small streams from a number of tributary valleys, it eventually disgorges into the North Sea at Whitby, the only estuary and sheltered harbour of any size between the Humber and the Tees.

Both nature and man have produced the present landscape of the North York Moors and as always the underlying rocks are the most important element. They belong to the relatively young Jurassic group, several layers of different rocks laid down roughly between 140 and 180 million years ago. Massive earth movements uplifted them from the sea bed, folding and tilting them to the south to create what is known at the 'Cleveland Dome'. Further earth movements, and the action of erosion and glaciation, fashioned them into their present pattern of hills and valleys. Because of the tilt to the south it is the oldest layers, the shales and ironstones of the Lower Jurassic, that have been exposed in the north, in the Cleveland Hills. The heartland of the Moors chiefly comprises the sandstones of the Middle Jurassic period, and in the Hambleton and Tabular Hills of the south are the limestones of the Upper Jurassic, the youngest rocks.

The more ill-drained sandstones resulted in bogs that gave rise to the peat cover, which in turn created the right conditions for the growth of heather. In contrast limestone is more permeable and in the south of the region is a typical limestone landscape, with streams sometimes disappearing and flowing underground to leave dry valleys on the surface. In this area the almost parallel valleys are separated by a series of flat-topped hills stretching from the Hambleton Hills to the coast – hence the name 'tabular' to describe their distinctive shape.

Glaciation made a major and decisive imprint on the landscape. As the glaciers retreated during the last Ice Age, they temporarily left behind huge lakes, from which currents of meltwater poured, gouging out deep valleys and gorges. The most prominent of these are Newton Dale and the Forge Valley. The action of water was also responsible for scooping out one of the most dramatic physical features of the Moors, the vast natural amphitheatre of the Hole of Horcum. In the east of the region glacial debris blocked the original eastward passage of the River Derwent, causing it to carve a new and more circuitous route to the North Sea by flowing southwards through the Forge Valley and then turning westwards across the Vale of Pickering to the Ouse and on to the Humber. Unusual relics of the Ice Age came to light in 1821 when, during quarrying operations in Kirk Dale, workmen accidentally came upon a cave containing bones that were later revealed as the remains of a wide variety of animals. These included elephant, rhinoceros, hyena, bear and hippopotamus – creatures not normally associated with North Yorkshire but which lived here before the last Ice Age when the climate was considerably warmer.

As a remote area of high moorland and deep valleys, bordered on three sides by hills and on the fourth by a sometimes turbulent sea, it is not surprising that solitude and isolation have been the most consistent characteristics of the North York Moors,

at least until the mining boom and the advent of the first tourists in the nineteenth century. Even today, in an age of fast travel, increasing leisure and mass tourism, it is these qualities, and of course the outstanding scenic beauty and great variety of historic monuments, that are the main attractions for visitors.

The multitude of early historic remains include Bronze Age burial mounds (called 'howes'), standing stones, circular enclosures (there is a fine one called Studford Ring above Ampleforth on the southern rim of the Moors) and linear earthworks. The latter often stretch for long distances, and because of the large areas that they enclose it is assumed that they were probably territorial boundaries rather

The fine Norman nave at Ingleby Greenhow

than defensive structures. A spectacular section of one of these is followed along the edge of Urra Moor on Walk 27.

The Roman Conquest had little impact and has left little physical evidence. Forts were built to the south at York and Malton, but to the Romans the Moors were a relatively inhospitable highland zone away from their main lines of north – south communications. The construction of a series of signal stations along the coast, however, led to the building of a cross-moorland road from near Malton to the coast. The foundations of this, which survive on Wheeldale Moor near Goathland, are

Mallyan Spout, near Goathland

one of the most important decisions in the history of English Christianity – the decision to follow the Roman rather than the Celtic Church.

The Danish invasions of the ninth century brought a temporary lapse into another 'dark age' and the temporary decline of Christianity, but after the initial raids and orgy of destruction the new invaders settled down to become farmers and traders. Following an agreement to partition England, made between Alfred the Great and the Danes, the North York Moors became part of the Danish-ruled territory, the 'Danelaw', and the numerous Danish place-name endings of -by and -thorpe are evidence of large-scale settlement throughout Yorkshire.

The Norman Conquest of 1066 was initially followed by widespread destruction – William the Conqueror's infamous and savage suppression of rebellion called the 'Harrying of the North' – but afterwards it ushered in an era of major change. Norman kings established castles on the edge of the Moors at Helmsley, Scarborough and Pickering. The latter was often used as a hunting lodge as most of the region to the north of Pickering was designated a royal forest, an area in which the king possessed sole hunting rights, protected by a harsh and extremely unpopular code of laws. A large proportion of the old Pickering Forest, mostly treeless open moorland in the Middle Ages, is now covered by a different kind of forest landscape – the conifer plantations of the Forestry Commission.

A monastic revival followed in the wake of the Norman conquerors. Over the next two centuries existing monasteries were rebuilt and new ones founded. The remoteness and solitude of the region particularly attracted the Cistercians, who founded their second monastery in England at Rievaulx (valley of the Rye) in 1131 and later another one nearby at Byland. The substantial and beautifully situated ruins of these are featured in the selection of walks, as are the other major monastic sites at Whitby, Guisborough and the uniquely interesting Carthusian remains of Mount Grace Priory near Osmotherley. The medieval monks were successful and enterprising businessmen – clearing

both impressive in themselves as well as being a rare example of an exposed Roman road.

Following the collapse of Roman power came the Dark Ages when the North York Moors were subjected to various waves of invaders, all of whom left a more permanent and significant impact on the area than the departing Romans. First came the Angles, penetrating into the region via the estuaries of the Humber and the Tees and the valleys of the Esk, Ouse and Derwent. They founded most of the present settlements, evidenced by the prevalence of their usual place-name endings of -ham, -ing, -ton, and -ley. Yorkshire was incorporated within the Anglian kingdom of Deira, later united with neighbouring Bernicia to create the kingdom of Northumbria, one of the most powerful states of Anglo-Saxon England and a bastion of early Christianity. Two monasteries were established at Lastingham and Whitby, their sites still occupied by outstanding churches. In 664 the great abbey at Whitby hosted the synod which made forests, reclaiming land, constructing drainage schemes and in particular developing large-scale and profitable sheep farming. In addition they initiated the industrial exploitation of the area, notably iron-mining, that was to reach its peak during the nineteenth century.

One constant problem was transport across these wild, open, sometimes misty, often featureless and frequently boggy moorlands. Although routeways, sometimes marked by crosses, existed before the Middle Ages, most of the stone-flagged causeways and marker posts built to aid travel across the moors have a monastic origin. Routes were needed to haul building materials and to link the monasteries with their various scattered estates and granges. Some of the medieval marker posts survive, though many have been restored or replaced. One of the oldest, Lilla Cross, stands on Fylingdales Moor close to the 'golf balls' of the early warning station, an interesting juxtaposition of the ancient and modern. A particularly fine collection stands above the head of Rosedale: Old Ralph, Young Ralph, Fat Betty, Marjorie Bradley — names that are rooted in local folklore.

Despite Henry VIII's closure of the monasteries in the 1530s agriculture continued to develop and commercial activity continued to increase, albeit slowly. More paved routeways over the moors — 'pannier ways' for packhorses — were constructed, crossing the rivers and streams by high-arched bridges. Two of the best-preserved and most picturesque of these bridges span the River Esk — Beggar's Bridge near Glaisdale and Duck Bridge below Danby Castle. The eighteenth and early nineteenth centuries were the great age of droving, when cattle were driven long distances on the hoof from Scotland, Wales and the North to the markets in the Midlands and the South. One of the finest surviving examples of a droving route is the Hambleton Drove Road, which follows the crest of the western escarpment of the Hambleton Hills and was part of a long-distance route from Scotland to London. This both pre-dated the age of droving and has survived it, now forming part of the Cleveland Way. Later came the coach roads; a particularly scenic one was constructed between Kirbymoorside and Stokesley, using a high-level route along the ridge (Rudland Rigg) that separates Bransdale from Farndale. The railway development of the nineteenth century had the biggest impact of all on the region, breaking down the isolation and remoteness of much of it for the first time.

The nineteenth century saw the heyday of mining in the North York Moors. Jet, alum and potash were all extracted but the major boom came in iron-mining. Stand on almost any point of the Cleveland escarpment looking northwards and the eye is inevitably drawn to the highly industrialised and built-up area of Teesside. Superficially there appears to be little in common between these quiet, thinly-populated moors and the noise and bustle of Middlesbrough but it was the presence of iron ore in the former that led to the growth of the latter, the archetypal Victorian boom town, and fuelled the iron and steel industries of Teesside.

The largest deposits were discovered in Rosedale and the major problem of how to transport the ore from that remote valley to the River Tees was solved by a feat of engineering, astonishing even by Victorian standards. A railway was built across the moors from the mines around Rosedale to the top of the Cleveland escarpment. From there the wagons were dropped 700 feet (213m) down the steep Ingleby Incline to the plain below from where they continued to the Tees. Following the decline of iron-mining in the area in the early twentieth century, the Rosedale Ironstone Railway closed in 1929, but remains of the iron mines can still be seen and the track makes an excellent high-level walking route (see Walk 16); the Ingleby Incline is descended in Walk 28.

It was not only for industrial purposes that railways were constructed; they also brought visitors into the area. The nineteenth century saw the start of the tourist industry, early visitors coming principally to view scenic wonders, such as the Hole of Horcum and the waterfalls around Goathland, or to admire historic remains like Rievaulx Abbey. Later came the influx of holidaymakers and day trippers from Teesside to enjoy the seaside delights of Scarborough, Whitby and smaller resorts such as Robin Hood's Bay. Railways were built connecting the coastal resorts with York and Middlesbrough and the main railway across the Moors linked Middlesbrough with Whitby via the Esk valley. From Grosmont a line ran southwards from the Esk valley, via the wooded gorge of Newton Dale, to provide a link with Pickering. Of these railways, the Esk Valley line survives, the link from Grosmont to Pickering is now the privately-owned North York Moors Railway (still running steam trains) and although the Whitby to Scarborough coastal route has gone, part of its track has been converted into an excellent footpath.

The twentieth century has brought a much greater influx of − mainly 'car borne' − tourists; it has also seen the planting of conifer plantations and the construction of the Fylingdales early warning station. Public attitudes to the last two developments, both controversial, have mellowed and changed: in both cases the initial hostility has been replaced by either a grudging acceptance or even a certain degree of affection. The conifers were planted by the Forestry Commission in the years after the First World War when the large plantations of Dalby, Wykeham, Cropton, Hambleton and Cleveland forests spread over a large area,

particularly in the eastern part of the Moors. The passage of time, more sensitive planting and the provision of amenities for visitors have helped to blunt much of the earlier criticism and now these forests are regarded by many as an additional asset rather than an alien intrusion into the landscape. Similarly the Fylingdales 'golf balls', put up in the 1960s and regarded as an unwelcome, even sinister, intrusion, have become accepted to the extent that there is resentment at plans to replace them by a pyramid. They can be regarded as the latest in a long line of defensive, early warning devices along this stretch of coast − part of a tradition that includes the Roman signal stations and the Norman castle at Scarborough.

It is this rich and varied heritage, combined with the splendid and equally varied scenery of coast, moor, hills, dales and forest, that makes the North York Moors a paradise for walkers. In this fine region you can walk along the Roman road over Wheeldale Moor, the Hambleton Drove Road, the old coach road over Rudland Rigg, and the Rosedale Ironstone Railway; you can follow parts of the Cleveland Way and you can visit Saxon churches, medieval castles and abbeys, lovely villages and sites of industrial archaeology. This tremendous variety can be enjoyed in the following selection of walks.

Idyllic coastal village of Runswick Bay

The National Parks and countryside recreation

Ten National Parks were created in England and Wales as a result of an Act of Parliament in 1949. In addition to these, there are numerous specially designated Areas of Outstanding Natural Beauty, Country and Regional Parks, Sites of Special Scientific Interest and picnic areas scattered throughout England, Wales and Scotland, all of which share the twin aims of preservation of the countryside and public accessibility and enjoyment.

In trying to define a National Park, one point to bear in mind is that unlike many overseas ones, Britain's National Parks are not owned by the nation. The vast bulk of the land in them is under private ownership. John Dower, whose report in 1945 created their framework, defined a National Park as 'an extensive area of beautiful and relatively wild country in which, for the nation's benefit and by appropriate national decision and action, (a) the characteristic landscape beauty is strictly preserved, (b) access and facilities for public open-air enjoyment are amply provided, (c) wildlife and buildings and places of architectural and historic interest are suitably protected, while (d) established farming use is effectively maintained'.

The concept of having designated areas of protected countryside grew out of a number of factors that appeared towards the end of the nineteenth century; principally greater facilities and opportunities for travel, the development of various conservationist bodies and the establishment of National Parks abroad. Apart from a few of the early individual travellers such as Celia Fiennes and Daniel Defoe, who were usually more concerned with commenting on agricultural improvements, the appearance of towns and the extent of antiquities to be found than with the wonders of nature, interest in the countryside as a source of beauty, spiritual refreshment and recreation, and, along with that, an interest in

conserving it, did not arise until the Victorian era. Towards the end of the eighteenth century, improvements in road transport enabled the wealthy to visit regions that had hitherto been largely inaccessible and, by the middle of the nineteenth century, the construction of the railways opened up such possibilities to the middle classes and, later on, to the working classes in even greater numbers. At the same time, the Romantic movement was in full swing and, encouraged by the works of Wordsworth, Coleridge and Shelley, interest and enthusiasm for wild places, including the mountain, moorland and hill regions of northern and western Britain, were now in vogue. Eighteenth-century taste had thought of the Scottish Highlands, the Lake District and Snowdonia as places to avoid, preferring controlled order and symmetry in nature as well as in architecture and town planning. But upper and middle class Victorian travellers were thrilled and awed by what they saw as the untamed savagery and wilderness of mountain peaks, deep and secluded gorges, thundering waterfalls, towering cliffs and rocky crags. In addition, there was a growing reaction against the materialism and squalor of Victorian industrialisation and urbanisation and a desire to escape from the formality and artificiality of town life into areas of unspoilt natural beauty.

A result of this was the formation of a number of different societies, all concerned with the 'great outdoors': naturalist groups, rambling clubs and conservationist organisations. One of the earliest of these was the Commons, Open Spaces and Footpaths Preservation Society, originally founded in 1865 to preserve commons and develop public access to the countryside. Particularly influential was the National Trust, set up in 1895 to protect and maintain both places of natural beauty and places of historic interest, and, later on, the Councils for the Preservation of Rural England, Wales and Scotland, three separate bodies that came into being between 1926 and 1928.

The world's first National Park was the Yellowstone Park in the United States, designated in 1872. This was followed by others in Canada, South Africa, Germany, Switzerland, New

Zealand and elsewhere, but in Britain such places did not come about until after the Second World War. Proposals for the creation of areas of protected countryside were made before the First World War and during the 1920s and 1930s, but nothing was done. The growing demand from people in towns for access to open country and the reluctance of landowners – particularly those who owned large expanses of uncultivated moorland – to grant it led to a number of ugly incidents, in particular the mass trespass in the Peak District in 1932, when fighting took place between ramblers and gamekeepers and some of the trespassers received stiff prison sentences.

It was in the climate exemplified by the Beveridge Report and the subsequent creation of the welfare state, however, that calls for countryside conservation and access came to fruition in parliament. Based on the recommendations of the Dower Report (1945) and the Hobhouse Committee (1947), the National Parks and Countryside Act of 1949 provided for the designation and preservation of areas both of great scenic beauty and of particular wildlife and scientific interest throughout Britain. More specifically it provided for the creation of National Parks in England and Wales. Scotland was excluded because, with greater areas of open space and a smaller population, there were fewer pressures on the Scottish countryside and therefore there was felt to be less need for the creation of such protected areas.

A National Parks Commission was set up, and over the next eight years ten areas were designated as parks; seven in England (Northumberland, Lake District, North York Moors, Yorkshire Dales, Peak District, Exmoor and Dartmoor) and three in Wales (Snowdonia, Brecon Beacons and Pembrokeshire Coast). At the same time the Commission was also given the responsibility for designating other smaller areas of high recreational and scenic qualities (Areas of Outstanding Natural Beauty), plus the power to propose and develop long-distance footpaths, now called National Trails,

though it was not until 1965 that the first of these, the Pennine Way, came into existence.

Further changes came with the Countryside Act of 1968 (a similar one for Scotland had been passed in 1967). The National Parks Commission was replaced by the Countryside Commission, which was now to oversee and review virtually all aspects of countryside conservation, access and provision of recreational amenities. The Country Parks, which were smaller areas of countryside often close to urban areas, came into being. A number of long-distance footpaths were created, followed by an even greater number of unofficial long- or middle-distance paths, devised by individuals, ramblers' groups or local authorities. Provision of car parks and visitor centres, way-marking of public rights of way and the production of leaflets giving suggestions for walking routes all increased, a reflection both of increased leisure and of a greater desire for recreational activity, of which walking in particular, now recognised as the most popular leisure pursuit, has had a great explosion of interest.

The authorities who administer the individual National Parks have the very difficult task of reconciling the interests of the people who live and earn their living within them with those of the visitors. National Parks, and the other designated areas, are not living museums. Developments of various kinds, in housing, transport and rural industries, are needed. There is pressure to exploit the resources of the area, through more intensive farming, or through increased quarrying and forestry, extraction of minerals or the construction of reservoirs.

In the end it all comes down to a question of balance; a balance between conservation and 'sensitive development'. On the one hand there is a responsibility to preserve and enhance the natural beauty of the National Parks and to promote their enjoyment by the public, and on the other, the needs and well-being of the people living and working in them have to be borne in mind.

Hutton-le-Hole, one of the prettiest of moors' villages

The National Trust

Anyone who likes visiting places of natural beauty and/or historic interest has cause to be grateful to the National Trust. Without it, many such places would probably have vanished by now, either under an avalanche of concrete and bricks and mortar or through reservoir construction or blanket afforestation.

It was in response to the pressures on the countryside posed by the relentless march of Victorian industrialisation that the Trust was set up in 1895. Its founders, inspired by the common goals of protecting and conserving Britain's national heritage and widening public access to it, were Sir Robert Hunter, Octavia Hill and Canon Rawnsley; a solicitor, a social reformer and a clergyman respectively. The latter was particularly influential. As a canon of Carlisle Cathedral and vicar of Crosthwaite (near Keswick), he was concerned about threats to the Lake District and had already been active in protecting footpaths and promoting public access to open countryside. After the flooding of Thirlmere in 1879 to create a large reservoir, he and his two colleagues became increasingly convinced that the only effective protection was outright ownership of land.

The purpose of the National Trust is to preserve areas of natural beauty and sites of historic interest by acquisition, holding them in trust for the nation and making them available for public access and enjoyment. Some of its properties have been acquired through purchase, but many have been donated. Nowadays it is one of the biggest landowners in the country and protects over half a million acres of land, including nearly 500 miles of coastline and a large number of historic properties (mostly houses) in England, Wales and Northern Ireland. (There is a separate National Trust for Scotland, which was set up in 1931.)

Furthermore, once a piece of land has come under Trust ownership, it is difficult for its status to be altered. As a result of Parliamentary legislation in 1907, the Trust was given the right to declare its property inalienable, so ensuring that in any dispute it can appeal directly to Parliament.

As it works towards its dual aims of conserving areas of attractive countryside and encouraging greater public access (not easy to reconcile in this age of mass tourism), the Trust provides an excellent service to walkers by creating new concessionary paths and waymarked trails, by maintaining stiles and footbridges and by combating the ever increasing problem of footpath erosion.

The Ramblers' Association

No organisation works more actively to protect and extend the rights and interests of walkers in the countryside than the Ramblers' Association. Its aims (summarised here) are clear: to foster a greater knowledge, love and care of the countryside; to assist in the protection and enhancement of public rights of way and areas of natural beauty; to work for greater public access to the countryside and to encourage more people to take up rambling as a healthy, recreational activity.

It was founded in 1935 when, following the setting up of a National Council of Ramblers' Federation in 1931, a number of federations earlier formed in London, Manchester, the Midlands and elsewhere came together to create a more effective pressure group, to deal with such contemporary problems as the disappearance and obstruction of footpaths, the prevention of access to open mountain and moorland and increasing hostility from landowners. This was the era of the mass trespasses, when there were sometimes violent confrontations between ramblers and gamekeepers, especially on the moorlands of the Peak District.

Since then the Ramblers' Association has played an influential role in preserving and developing the national footpath network, supporting the creation of National Parks and encouraging the designation and way-marking of long-distance footpaths.

Our freedom to walk in the countryside is precarious, and requires constant vigilance. As well as the perennial problems of footpaths being illegally obstructed, disappearing through lack of use or extinguished by housing or road construction, new dangers can spring up at any time.

It is to meet such problems and dangers that the Ramblers' Association exists and represents the interests of all walkers. The address to write to for information on the Ramblers' Association and how to become a member is given on page 78.

Walkers and the law

The average walker in a National Park or other popular walking area, armed with the appropriate Ordnance Survey map, reinforced perhaps by a guidebook giving detailed walking instructions, is unlikely to run into legal difficulties, but it is useful to know something about the law relating to public rights of way. The right to walk over certain parts of the countryside has developed over a long period of time, and how such rights came into being and how far they are protected by the law is a complex subject, fascinating in its own right, but too lengthy to be discussed here. The following comments are intended simply to be a helpful guide, backed up by the Countryside Access Charter, a concise summary of walkers' rights and obligations drawn up by the Countryside Commission.

Basically there are two main kinds of public rights of way: footpaths (for walkers only) and bridle-ways (for walkers, riders on horseback and pedal cyclists). Footpaths and bridle-ways are shown by broken green lines on Ordnance Survey Pathfinder and Outdoor Leisure maps and broken red lines on Landranger maps. There is also a third category, called byways or 'roads used as a public path': chiefly broad, walled tracks (green lanes) or farm roads, which walkers, riders and cyclists have to share, usually only occasionally, with motor vehicles. Many of these public paths have been in existence for hundreds of years and some even originated as prehistoric trackways and have been in constant use for well over 2,000 years.

The term 'right of way' means exactly what it says. It gives right of passage over what, in the vast majority of cases, is private land, and you are required to keep to the line of the path and not stray onto the land either side. If you inadvertently wander off the right of way – either because of faulty map-reading or because the route is not clearly indicated on the ground – you are technically trespassing and the wisest course is to ask the nearest available person (farmer or fellow walker) to direct you back to the correct route. There are stories of unpleasant confrontations between walkers and farmers at times, but in general most farmers are helpful and co-operative when responding to a genuine and polite request for assistance in route finding.

Obstructions can sometimes be a problem and probably the commonest of these is where a path across a field has been ploughed up. It is legal for a farmer to plough up a path provided that he restores it within two weeks, barring exceptionally bad weather. This does not always happen and here the walker is presented with a dilemma. Does he follow the line of the path, even if this inevitably means treading on crops, or does he use his common sense and walk around the edge of the field? The latter course of action often seems the best but, as this means that you would be trespassing, you are, in law, supposed to keep to the exact line of the path, avoiding unnecessary damage to crops. In the case of other obstructions which may block a path (illegal fences and locked gates etc.), common sense again has to be used in order to negotiate them by the easiest method (detour or removal), followed by reporting the matter to the local council or National Park authority.

Apart from rights of way enshrined by law, there are a number of other paths available to walkers. Permissive or concessionary paths have been created where a landowner has given permission for the public to use a particular route across his land. The main problem with these is that, as they have been granted as a concession, there is no legal right to use them and therefore they can be extinguished at any time. In practice, many of these concessionary routes have been

Bransdale

established on land owned either by large public bodies such as the Forestry Commission or the water authorities, or by a private one, such as the National Trust, and as these mainly encourage walkers to use their paths, they are unlikely to be closed unless a change of ownership occurs.

Walkers also have free access to Country Parks (except where requested to keep away from certain areas for ecological reasons e.g. wildlife protection, woodland regeneration, safeguarding of rare plants etc.), canal towpaths and most beaches. By custom, though not by right, you are generally free to walk across the open and uncultivated higher land of mountain, moorland and fell, but this varies from area to area and from one season to another — grouse moors, for example, will be out of bounds during the breeding and shooting seasons and some open areas are used as Ministry of Defence firing ranges, for which reason access will be restricted. In some areas the situation has been clarified as a result of 'access agreements' between the landowners and either the county council or the National Park authority, which clearly define when and where you can walk over such open country.

Countryside Access Charter

Your rights of way are:
- Public footpaths — on foot only. Sometimes waymarked in yellow
- Bridle-ways — on foot, horseback and pedal cycle. Sometimes waymarked in blue
- Byways (usually old roads), most 'roads used as public paths' and, of course, public roads — all traffic has the right of way

Use maps, signs and waymarks to check rights of way. Ordnance Survey Pathfinder and Landranger maps show most public rights of way

On rights of way you can:
- take a pram, pushchair or wheelchair if practicable
- take a dog (on a lead or under close control)
- take a short route round an illegal obstruction or remove it sufficiently to get past

You have a right to go for recreation to:
- public parks and open spaces — on foot
- most commons near older towns and cities — on foot and sometimes on horseback
- private land where the owner has a formal agreement with the local authority

In addition you can use the following by local or established custom or consent, but ask for advice if you are unsure:
- many areas of open country, such as moorland, fell and coastal areas, especially those in the care of the National Trust, and some commons
- some woods and forests, especially those owned by the Forestry Commission
- Country Parks and picnic sites
- most beaches
- canal towpaths
- some private paths and tracks

Consent sometimes extends to horse-riding and cycling

For your information:
- county councils and London boroughs maintain and record rights of way, and register commons
- obstructions, dangerous animals, harassment and misleading signs on rights of way are illegal and you should report them to the county council
- paths across fields can be ploughed, but must normally be reinstated within two weeks
- landowners can require you to leave land to which you have no right of access
- motor vehicles are normally permitted only on roads, byways and some 'roads used as public paths'

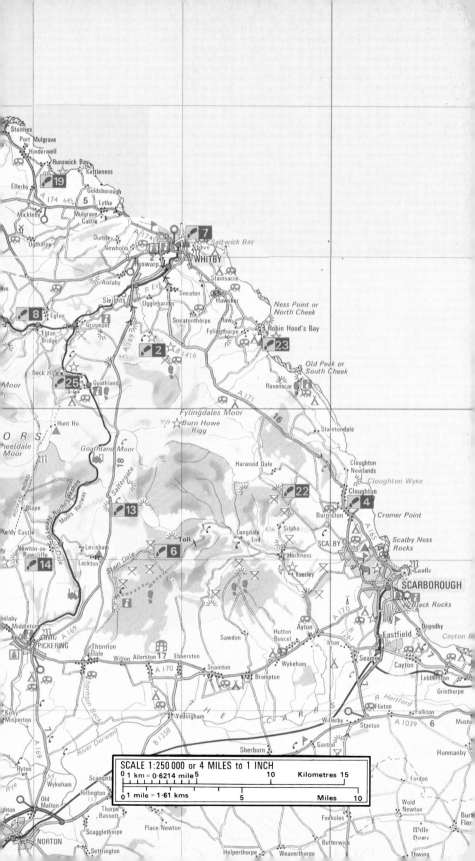

CONVENTIONAL SIGNS

1:25 000 or 2½ INCHES to 1 MILE

ROADS AND PATHS

Not necessarily rights of way

M I or A 6(M)	M I or A 6(M)	Motorway
A 31 (T)	A 31 (T)	Trunk road
A 35	A 35	Main road
B 3074	B 3074	Secondary road
A 35	A 35	Dual carriageway
		Road generally more than 4m wide
		Road generally less than 4m wide
		Other road, drive or track

Narrow roads with passing places are annotated

Unfenced roads and tracks are shown by pecked lines

Path

RAILWAYS

	Multiple track } Standard gauge
	Single track
	Narrow gauge
	Siding
	Cutting
	Embankment
	Tunnel
	Road over & under
	Level crossing; station

PUBLIC RIGHTS OF WAY

Public rights of way may not be evident on the ground

| Public paths { Footpath | + + + + + Byway open to all traffic |
| Bridleway | Road used as a public path |

The indication of a towpath in this book does not necessarily imply a public right of way
The representation of any other road, track or path is no evidence of the existence of a right of way

BOUNDARIES

— · — · — · —	County (England and Wales)
— — — — —	District
⊶ ⊶ ⊶ ⊶ ⊶	London Borough
·············	Civil Parish (England)* Community (Wales)
— — — — — —	Constituency (County, Borough, Burgh or European Assembly)

Coincident boundaries are shown by the first appropriate symbol

*For Ordnance Survey purposes County Boundary is deemed to be the limit of the parish structure whether or not a parish area adjoins

SYMBOLS

♦	Place	with tower
♦	of	with spire, minaret or dome
+	worship	without such additions
⌗ △		Glasshouse; youth hostel
		Bus or coach station
⚓ ⚑ ⋏		Lighthouse; lightship; beacon
△		Triangulation station
	Triangulation point on	church or chapel
		lighthouse, beacon
		building; chimney
pylon pole		Electricity transmission line

VILLA	Roman antiquity (AD 43 to AD 420)
Castle	Other antiquities
✛	Site of antiquity
⚔ 1066	Site of battle (with date)
	Gravel pit
	Sand pit
	Chalk pit, clay pit or quarry
	Refuse or slag heap
	Sloping wall

	Water	Mud
	Sand; sand & shingle	
	National Park or Forest Park Boundary	
NT	National Trust open access	
NT	National Trust limited access	
NTS NTS	National Trust for Scotland	

Surface heights are to the nearest metre above mean sea level. Heights shown close to a triangulation pillar refer to the ground level height at the pillar and not necessarily the summit.

VEGETATION

Limits of vegetation are defined by positioning of the symbols but may be delineated also by pecks or dots

	Coniferous trees		Orchard	Bracken, rough grassland
	Non-coniferous trees		Scrub	In some areas bracken ( ) and rough grassland ( ) are shown separately
	Coppice		Marsh, reeds, saltings	Heath

Shown collectively as rough grassland on some sheets

In some areas reeds ( ) and saltings ( ) are shown separate

HEIGHTS AND ROCK FEATURES

| 50 | Determined | ground survey |
| 285 | by | air survey |

Vertical face

Loose rock   Boulders   Outcrop   Scree

Contours are at 5 metres vertical interval

TOURIST INFORMATION

Abbey, Cathedral, Priory	Garden	Other tourist feature
Aquarium	Golf course or links	Picnic site
Camp site	Historic house	Preserved railway
Caravan site	Information centre	Racecourse
Castle	Motor racing	Skiing
Cave	Museum	Viewpoint
Country park	Nature or forest trail	Wildlife park
Craft centre	Nature reserve	Zoo
Parking		
Public Convenience (in rural areas)	**Castle** / SAILING — Selected places of interest	
Ancient Monuments and Historic Buildings in the care of the Secretary of State for the Environment which are open to the public.	T — Public telephone	
	Mountain rescue post	
National trail or Recreational Path Long Distance Route (Scotland only)	NATIONAL PARK ACCESS LAND — Boundary of National Park access land	
	Private land for which the National Park Planning Board have negotiated public access	
nnine Way — Named path	Access Point	

ABBREVIATIONS   1:25 000 or 2½ INCHES to 1 MILE also 1:10 000/1:10 560 or 6 INCHES to 1 MILE

P,BS	Boundary Post or Stone	P	Post Office	A,R	Telephone, AA or RAC
H	Club House	Pol Sta	Police Station	TH	Town Hall
V	Ferry Foot or Vehicle	PC	Public Convenience	Twr	Tower
B	Foot Bridge	PH	Public House	W	Well
O	House	Sch	School	Wd Pp	Wind Pump
P,MS	Mile Post or Stone	Spr	Spring		
on	Monument	T	Telephone, public		

Abbreviations applicable only to 1:10 000/1:10 560 or 6 INCHES to 1 MILE

h	Church	GP	Guide Post	TCB	Telephone Call Box
Sta	Fire Station	P	Pole or Post	TCP	Telephone Call Post
	Fountain	S	Stone	Y	Youth Hostel

WALKS

1 Start point of walk	Featured walk	Route of walk	Alternative route

FOLLOW THE COUNTRY CODE
Enjoy the countryside and respect its life and work

Guard against all risk of fire	Take your litter home
Fasten all gates	Help to keep all water clean
Keep your dogs under close control	Protect wildlife, plants and trees
Keep to public paths across farmland	Take special care on country roads
Leave livestock, crops and machinery alone	Make no unnecessary noise
Use gates and stiles to cross fences, hedges and walls	

Reproduced by permission of the Countryside Commission

1 Rievaulx Abbey

Start:	Rievaulx Abbey
Distance:	3 miles (4.75 km)
Approximate time:	1½ hours
Parking:	Parking areas beside the lane just below the abbey
Refreshments:	None
Ordnance Survey maps:	Landranger 100 (Malton & Pickering) and Outdoor Leisure 26 (North York Moors — Western area)

General description *The glorious and mellow ruins of Rievaulx Abbey, in sight for most ot the way, form the focal point of this delightful walk in Ryedale, across fields, through woods and along lanes. Although a short walk, it is worth taking time over, both for its own sake and for the opportunity to thoroughly explore the abbey either at the beginning or end.*

By any standards Rievaulx is one of the most magnificent monastic remains in the country — perhaps the finest of all, combining the completeness and architectural qualities of Fountains with the picturesque setting of Bolton, its two great Yorkshire rivals. Founded in 1131 by Walter l'Espec, lord of nearby Helmsley, it was the first Cistercian monastery in northern England, soon becoming one of the largest and most prosperous, as can be seen from its surviving buildings. Its wealth came from owning vast areas of land and acquiring large profits from various commercial activities, principally sheep farming and iron-mining. The enterprising Rievaulx monks even diverted the River Rye, which originally ran along the eastern side of the valley close to the abbey, to its present course along the western side, thus gaining extra grazing land. At its height Rievaulx housed more than 600 monks and lay brothers, but like most other monasteries it declined, and at its dissolution in 1539 it only had about twenty-two.

The abbey was built in the second half of the twelfth century but most of the existing remains — transepts and east end of the church, refectory, large infirmary hall and dormitory — date from an extensive re-building programme in the early thirteenth century and are superb examples of Early English architecture. The east end of the church is almost complete and looks most majestic as you walk between the aisles, with the sun glinting on the pale stonework and casting shadows across its now grassy floor.

Walk up the lane by the little River Rye on the left, passing the ruins of the abbey. On the ridge to the right the classical temples on Rievaulx Terrace can be seen. The terrace

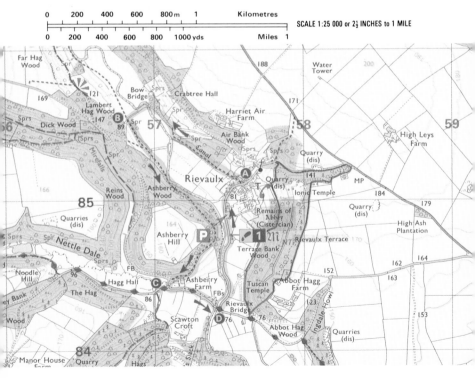

0	200	400	600	800 m	1		Kilometres	
0	200	400	600	800	1000 yds		Miles 1	

SCALE 1:25 000 or 2½ INCHES to 1 MILE

The incomparable setting of Rievaulx Abbey

was laid out and the imitation temples erected in the eighteenth century by Thomas Duncombe (from nearby Duncombe Park) as an appropriate setting from which to view the abbey below, at a time when ruins of all kinds were very fashionable with the English aristocracy. Continue through the tiny but charming village and, at a footpath sign to Bow Bridge **(A)**, turn left and walk across to a gate. Go through and follow the path across a field, heading towards a fence and hedge on the right and keeping by them to a stile. Climb over and continue, by a wire fence and line of trees on the right, to another stile. The shallow canal to the right was once part of the water supply to the abbey.

Climb the stile, and another one a few yards ahead, to rejoin the River Rye, keeping along its banks for a short while before bearing right to climb a stile at a footpath sign. Turn left along a rough track, cross Bow Bridge, an attractive old pack-horse

bridge, and keep ahead to the base of the wooded hill in front **(B)**. Here turn left through a gate, at a footpath sign to Ashberry, and continue over a stile and through another gate. Now the path starts to ascend the wooded slopes of Ashberry Hill above the River Rye, and all the way along, especially from the highest points, the views to the left across to the abbey ruins in their sheltered setting, backed by the wooded slopes of Rievaulx Bank and topped by the classical temple on Rievaulx Terrace, are especially memorable – the highlight of the walk. Later the path flattens out and then descends, with fine views over Ryedale, passing through a gate and continuing by the right-hand side of Ashberry Farm to a lane.

Turn left, cross a bridge, and turn left again **(C)** (signposted Helmsley and Rievaulx) to follow a lane for ¼ mile (0.5 km) down to Rievaulx Bridge **(D)**. Cross it and turn left back to the starting point, with more outstanding views of the abbey.

19

2 Falling Foss and Littlebeck

Start:	Forestry Commission car park at Falling Foss
Distance:	3 ½ miles (5.5 km)
Approximate time:	2 hours
Parking:	Falling Foss
Refreshments:	None
Ordnance Survey maps:	Landranger 94 (Whitby) and Outdoor Leisure 27 (North York Moors − Eastern area)

General description *A dramatic waterfall, farmland, a tiny and remote hamlet and a* most delightful wooded gorge − plus views of surrounding moorland and conifer forests − are the main ingredients packed into this short but most attractive and varied walk. For the most part the terrain is undemanding, though there is some climbing along the side of the gorge south of Littlebeck.

Turn left out of the car park down a broad wooded track, signposted to Falling Foss, and bear right away from the track to view the fall, a most impressive sight. Cross a footbridge over the beck, bear left up to a bridge ahead and, on the right-hand side of the bridge, turn right **(A)** to rejoin the track that soon climbs out of the wooded valley, with fine views over open country and moorland to the right. After passing farm

Falling Foss

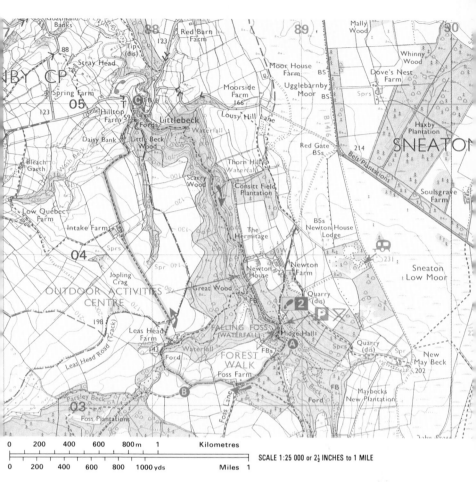

```
0    200   400   600   800 m   1        Kilometres
0    200   400   600   800  1000 yds        Miles   1
```

SCALE 1:25 000 or 2½ INCHES to 1 MILE

buildings on the right, continue through two gates in quick succession and keep ahead to a junction of tracks **(B)**. Turn right here through a gate and walk along a clear path which after a while descends gently between hedge-banks and a stream on the left to go through a gate. Cross the stream, continue through another gate into the farmyard of Leas Head Farm, turning sharp left at a yellow waymark and passing through a metal gate.

Continue along a track which curves to the right and goes gently uphill to another metal gate. From here the views are superb all round — forest behind, moorland to the left, the Esk valley ahead and the wooded gorge of Littlebeck to the right. Go through the gate, continue through two more metal gates and on through a farmyard. At the end of the farm buildings, turn right and then left to pass through another metal gate and along a tarmac farm road. Keep along this road for about ¾ mile (1.25 km) as it bends first right, then left and drops into the valley to the hamlet of Littlebeck.

Where the farm road bends right to descend to a road junction, keep ahead along a narrow path which crosses a footbridge and continues by the left-hand side of Littlebeck Methodist Chapel to the road **(C)**. Cross over and take the path opposite between trees and hedges which, after 50 yards (46 m), turns right over another footbridge. Bear slightly right for a few yards along the uphill road ahead, looking out for a public footpath sign on the right by a bench. Here go through a gate marked 'Falling Foss' and follow a narrow but clear path along the left-hand side of the beck through a delightful, steep-sided, thickly-wooded ravine. The path turns right, climbs a flight of steps to pass across the top of a cave, and continues up and down through this beautiful woodland, at one stage climbing steps to the top edge of the ravine by a cave called The Hermitage. Near the end of the walk the path forks — here you can either bear right downhill to view Falling Foss again, or take the left-hand fork which curves left and heads uphill directly back to the car park.

21

3 Farndale

Start:	Low Mill
Distance:	4 miles (6.5 km)
Approximate time:	2 hours
Parking:	Low Mill
Refreshments:	Pub at Church Houses
Ordnance Survey maps:	Landranger 94 (Whitby) and 100 (Malton & Pickering), Outdoor Leisure 26 (North York Moors — Western area)

General description *This enchanting walk, initially across the meadows and through the woods that line the banks of the little River Dove from Low Mill to Church Houses, and later returning by field paths along the edge of Farndale, is known as the 'Daffodil Walk' as in spring the banks of the river are a glorious riot of yellow. Although obviously at its best when the daffodils are out, this is a lovely walk at any time of the year.*

From the car park take the path opposite the post office (public footpath sign to High Mill) down to a footbridge **(A)**. Cross over and turn left through a gate to follow the banks of the River Dove for 1½ miles (2.5 km) to High Mill — keep by the river all the while, through gates and over stiles, across meadows and through woods that are carpeted with daffodils in spring. It is difficult to conceive of a finer stretch of riverside walking, and it is further enhanced by the superb views up Farndale.

Pass through the disused High Mill buildings and continue along a track (ignoring a public footpath sign to the left) for just over another ¼ mile (0.5 km) to the

April in Farndale — the 'Daffodil Walk'

hamlet of Church Houses **(B)**. Turn right by the pub along a lane signposted to Hutton-le-Hole and Castleton, soon bearing right again (signposted Hutton-le-Hole and Gillamoor). Follow the curving lane uphill for ½ mile (0.75 km), passing the small simple church on the left and, just past a house on the right, turn right through a gate **(C)**, at a public footpath sign, and walk along the edge of a field to another footpath sign about 100 yards (92 m) ahead. Having gained some height, there are now excellent views over Farndale for the remainder of the walk.

Turn left over a ladder stile at the footpath sign and follow the edge of a field, by a hedge on the right, to a gate. Go through and head towards a farm, keeping to the left of the farm buildings and passing through two more gates and along a broad track. Bear

right at a footpath sign, following its directions across the field towards the next farm, climb steps in the wall ahead and continue, by the farmhouse on the right, to a gate. Go through, keep ahead to climb a stile and walk across a field to a ladder stile. Climb over and continue through a gate by a footpath sign and along the edge of a field, by a hedge and fence on the left. Pass through another gate and keep along the edge of the next field, this time with the hedge and fence on the right, continuing through another gate and along a track to a farm. In the farmyard turn right through a gate and follow the path ahead, by a wall on the right, to climb a stile. Cross a stream and continue downhill along a partially paved path to Low Mill, where you cross the footbridge to return to the car park.

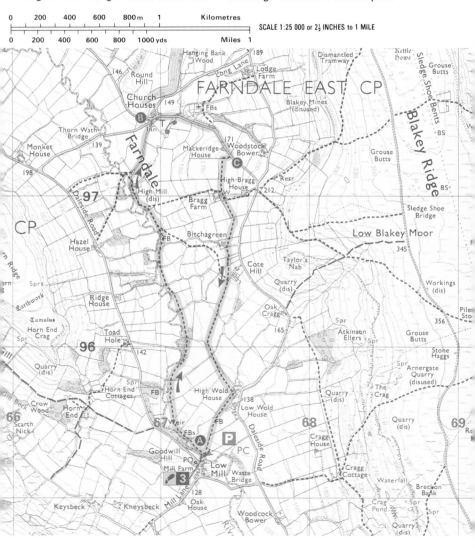

SCALE 1:25 000 or 2½ INCHES to 1 MILE

4 Cloughton and Hayburn Wykes

Start:	Cloughton
Distance:	4½ miles (7.25 km)
Approximate time:	2 hours
Parking:	Parking area opposite Court Green Farm (turn right at crossroads in Cloughton)
Refreshments:	Pubs in Cloughton, hotel at Hayburn Wyke
Ordnance Survey maps:	Landranger 101 (Scarborough & Bridlington) and Outdoor Leisure 27 (North York Moors – Eastern area)

General description *'Wyke' is a local word for a small, sheltered bay, and this walk takes you along a particularly attractive stretch of* the North Yorkshire coast between two such bays. The first half is along the coastal path itself and the return follows the track of the disused Whitby – Scarborough railway, now converted into a pleasant, shady footpath. Not only is the route easy to follow, it is also easy on the legs – despite some 'ups and downs' on the coastal path and, following the descent to the beach at Hayburn Wyke, the return ascent.

At the crossroads in the village of Cloughton on the main Whitby – Scarborough coast road, turn down the lane towards the sea. Pass Court Green Farm on the left and continue over the disused railway bridge (**A**) and ahead for ½ mile (0.75 km) to reach the coast at Cloughton Wyke. To the right the view is dominated by the headland on which stand the gaunt but imposing ruins of Scarborough Castle.

Where the lane ends at a small parking area above Cloughton Wyke, bear left to join the coastal path, part of the Cleveland Way (**B**). The route to Hayburn Wyke hugs the top of

SCALE 1:25 000 or 2½ INCHES to 1 MILE

The stony beach at Hayburn Wyke

the cliffs and involves a lot of climbing up and down steps, but there are some superb coastal views in both directions: Scarborough, Filey Brigg and even Flamborough Head can be seen behind, and in front there are glimpses of rocky and inaccessible beaches below, through the trees and gorse bushes that at times enclose the narrow path. After a fairly steep climb, the path levels out to give a grand view of Hayburn Wyke ahead.

Climb a stile and descend through Hayburn Wyke Woods, a nature reserve managed by the National Trust and Yorkshire Naturalists Trust, to a junction of paths and Cleveland Way signpost. Turn right here and continue through these lovely woods, bearing left and descending to the stony beach at Hayburn Wyke, near the side of a small waterfall where Hayburn Beck tumbles over gritstone boulders to reach the North Sea **(C)**.

Numerous fossils have been found on the beach here.

Retrace your steps up through the woods to the path junction and Cleveland Way sign and then keep straight ahead to a stile and National Trust sign. Climb over and continue across a field, turning right to a gate and another stile. Climb that and walk along the path ahead to the Hayburnwyke Hotel, turning sharp left at the hotel along a tarmac lane. After 100 yards (92 m) turn left again through a gate **(D)** to join the track of disused Yorkshire Coast Railway, completed in 1885 and formerly linking Whitby and Scarborough. Continue along this pleasant tree-lined route for 1 ½ miles (2.5 km), with more good views of the coast looking towards Scarborough, finally climbing up steps by the side of a bridge to go through a gate at the top **(A)**. Turn right along the lane back to Cloughton.

5 Kirk Dale

Start:	St Gregory's Minster, Kirk Dale
Distance:	4½ miles (7.25 km)
Approximate time:	2 hours
Parking:	Park in lane near church (*not* the church car park)
Refreshments:	None
Ordnance Survey maps:	Landranger 94 (Whitby) and 100 (Malton & Pickering) and Outdoor Leisure 26 (North York Moors — Western area)

General description *This is an easy-paced walk amidst the gentle landscape of Kirk Dale (the lower part of Bransdale), by Hodge Beck, through two wooded valleys and across farmland, with a fine old church as the focal point. From these southern fringes of the Moors, there are extensive views southwards across the Vale of Pickering to the Howardian Hills and the line of the Wolds.*

Start by walking down the lane to St Gregory's Minster, which occupies a beautiful, isolated position in the peaceful wooded valley of Hodge Beck. This is an ancient, most attractive and distinctive church whose origins can be traced back to Saxon times. Probably founded in the seventh century by monks from Lindisfarne, it is called a minster because it would have been the centre of missionary activities (mission house) in the early days of Christianity. There is, however, some dispute as to whether it was this church, rather than the one at nearby Lastingham, that was founded by St Cedd and in which he was buried. At any rate it contains some Saxon features — notably the west door, gravestones and the uniquely complete and well-preserved sundial over the south porch. After suffering destruction during the Danish invasions, the church was restored in the mid-eleventh century, just prior to the Norman Conquest, by Orm, a local landowner — his name ironically suggesting that he was probably of Viking origin. A detailed inscription on the sundial records this event.

Go through a gate in front of the church and walk along a path by the edge of a wood on the left. Cross Hodge Beck, continue ahead, drawing towards the trees on the right, and go through a gate to enter the wood, with the stream below on the left. Just after the track veers slightly to the right, turn left through a metal gate into a field and continue along the edge of the field, below the slopes of Thin Oaks Wood on the right, through a very pleasant valley. At the end of

St Gregory's Minster — fascinating church in a lovely setting

the field, turn right through a gate into the wood along a path parallel to Hodge Beck. The path starts to ascend, giving good views up Kirk Dale and, on meeting another path on the right, turn sharply (almost a U-turn) onto this path (A), continuing to ascend. At the next meeting of paths, near the top, turn left along a narrow path between gorse bushes for a few yards to a gate and yellow waymark. Turn right through the gate and head straight across a field, now emerging into open country with fine views to the right across the Vale of Pickering. At the far end of the field, turn left and keep by the field edge up to a gate in the far right-hand corner. Turn right through that gate and follow the edge of the next field round towards the buildings of Low Hagg Farm in front, turning left over a stile at a yellow waymark just before reaching the buildings. Continue across the next field, keeping the farm on the right, to climb another stile onto a lane (B).

Turn left along the lane for ¼ mile (0.5 km), take the first turning on the right, passing in front of High Hagg Farm, and continue towards a belt of woodland. The lane descends slightly and, at a public footpath sign on the right (C), turn sharp right through a gate and, for the next mile (1.5 km), follow a grassy path through the narrow, attractive, wooded valley of Robin Hood's Howl, ignoring all paths to the right and left. Eventually the valley becomes less steep, broadens out, and you arrive at a gate. Ahead is another lovely view across the Vale of Pickering. Go through the gate, keep ahead to a fence corner and, with a wire fence on the right, continue to a gate at the far end of the field. Go through to a junction of lanes (D) and keep ahead along the lane signposted to Kirk Dale and Helmsley, passing on the right Kirk Dale Cave, an old quarry where in 1821 the remains of a great variety of prehistoric animals – including hyena, bison, mammoth, elephants and rhinoceros – were found. Continue over Hodge Beck and back to the starting point above St Gregory's Minster.

6 The Bride Stones

Start:	Staindale Lake car park (reached along Dalby Forest Drive — toll payable)
Distance:	4½ miles (7.25 km)
Approximate time:	2½ hours
Parking:	Staindale Lake
Refreshments:	None
Ordnance Survey maps:	Landranger 94 (Whitby) and 101 (Scarborough & Bridlington), Outdoor Leisure 27 (North York Moors — Eastern area)

General description *The Bride Stones are two groups of rocks that stand out prominently amidst a striking landscape of bright green meadows and the dark green conifer woodlands of Dalby Forest which, but for the moors beyond, has at times a Canadian or Scandinavian feel. Within a modest distance there is a great variety of scenery — natural woodland, moorland and farmland, as well as conifer plantations — and only a few relatively gentle climbs are encountered.*

On the north side of the car park, go up three steps and walk across the grass to pick up a path near a National Trust sign. Much of this walk is through the Bridestones Nature Reserve, owned by the National Trust and managed jointly with the Yorkshire Naturalists Trust. Ahead are two stiles —

Low Bride Stones — sandstone outcrops amidst conifer forest

climb over the one on the right, and in a few yards, where the path forks, bear left to climb through the very attractive Low Wood, most of which is a natural oak wood. At the top bear right onto open moorland and the Low Bride Stones are just a short distance ahead.

The Low Bride Stones are probably more impressive than the High Bride Stones. Both are sandstone outcrops that have been fashioned into most fantastic shapes because the action of the weather has eroded the weaker layers of rock faster than the stronger layers. The name is derived from a Norse word meaning 'brink' or 'edge' stones. The view from the Low Bride Stones across forest and moor is outstanding and the High Bride Stones can be seen to the right across the valley of Bridestone Griff. Continue past the stones to a yellow waymark **(A)**. Here you can make a detour if you wish for a closer inspection of the High Bride Stones by continuing across the head of Bridestone Griff; otherwise bear right across heathery moorland towards the conifer woods ahead, turning left onto a broad track and keeping along it, by the edge of the conifers on the right, for about ½ mile (0.75 km). Just before a gate **(B)**, turn left along a faint path across the heather, making for a wire fence on the right and following that fence to a pond. Negotiate some rough grass near the pond to reach a stile, climb over and turn left along a track across Grime Moor. Over to the left the High Bride Stones stand out clearly, with the Low Bride Stones and dark conifer forest behind.

Shortly before reaching a farm, turn right over a stile in a wire fence **(C)** and head across a field, making for the corner of a wire fence on the left near another pond. Turn left to keep by the wire fence on the left, later veering right away from it and downhill to climb a stile in the far corner of the field. Continue diagonally across the middle of the next field, turning left along the edge of it to a lane **(D)**. Turn left along the lane heading downhill and turn left again, at a public footpath sign, along a track past Low Pastures Farm. Keep ahead at a National Trust sign (Bridestones), descending through woodland to climb a stile and continue along the track, turning right on approaching a farm and then left in front of the farm. Now follow the grassy track ahead, dropping down over a stream and continuing along the bottom edge of Low Wood, by a wire fence on the left, to a stile. Climb over and return to the car park a few yards ahead.

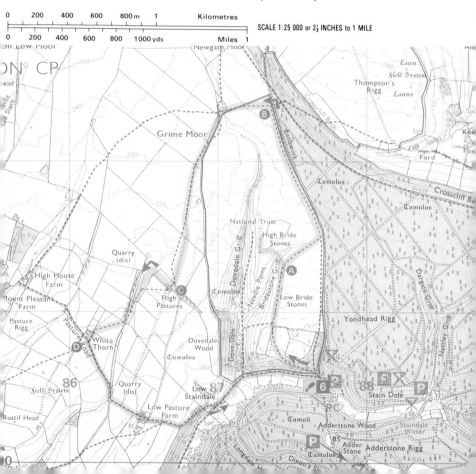

SCALE 1:25 000 or 2½ INCHES to 1 MILE

7 Whitby and Saltwick Bay

Start:	Whitby
Distance:	5 miles (8 km)
Approximate time:	2 ½ hours
Parking:	Whitby
Refreshments:	Restaurants, pubs and cafés in Whitby
Ordnance Survey maps:	Landranger 94 (Whitby) and Outdoor Leisure 27 (North York Moors – Eastern area)

General description *A short walk, but one that includes some spectacular coastal scenery, almost constant views of Whitby Abbey and the opportunity to explore one of the most fascinating of old towns. By following an anti-clockwise direction, you gain the advantage of descending rather than ascending the well-known 199 steps at Whitby that link the harbour with the church and abbey ruins on the cliff above.*

The long and varied history of Whitby – one of the cradles of English Christianity, fishing and whaling port, centre for shipbuilding, alum and jet industries and popular holiday resort – is reflected in its many fine buildings of all ages. A walk around its streets is an interesting and rewarding experience.

Until the coming of the railway in 1836 it was largely isolated from the rest of the country by the surrounding moors – hence its dependence on the sea. The young James Cook made his first voyage from Whitby and he used Whitby-built ships on his later, momentous voyages of discovery.

The two oldest buildings, the parish church and the abbey, stand on the East Cliff and are passed at the end of the walk. The sturdy-looking church, dating from the twelfth century, has been restored several times and is noted for its attractive interior, with its rare eighteenth-century panelling and pews. Nearby the splendid remains of Whitby Abbey dominate both the town and surrounding area. The original abbey, a mixed community of monks and nuns, was founded in 657 by St Hilda and hosted the famous Synod at Whitby in 664 when the English Church, torn between the different practices of Roman and Celtic Christianity, decided to follow the Roman Church. Its exposed position high up on the cliffs made it highly vulnerable and it was destroyed during Viking raids. The present imposing ruins, mainly of the church, date mostly from the thirteenth century and the best-preserved parts are the east end and the striking north transept, the latter almost intact and standing to its full height.

SCALE 1:25 000 or 2½ INCHES to 1 MILE

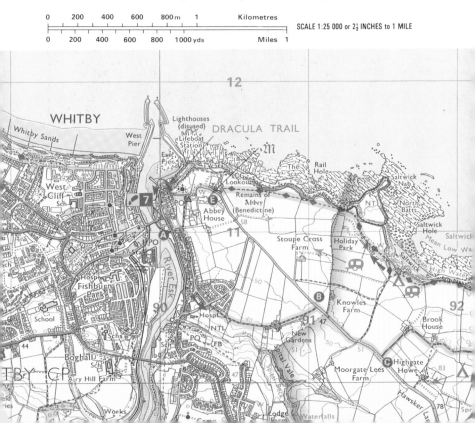

Whitby — river, harbour, church and abbey ruins

The walk starts by the harbour at the eastern end of the bridge over the River Esk. With your back to the sea, walk along the road by the side of the river, shortly turning left **(A)** to climb some steps up Boulby Bank, and continue along a cobbled path between houses to a road. Walk along to a crossroads and continue up some more steps opposite and along a flagged path to join a lane. Keep along this lane, past houses and through farm buildings, to go through a gate and continue along a path to a road **(B)**.

Turn right for nearly ½ mile (0.75km) and, at signs to Whitby Lighthouse, Brook House and several other farmhouses, turn left along a farm road **(C)**. Over to the left is a fine view of the abbey. Keep along this farm road for 1 mile (1.5 km), following it to the right after passing through a farmyard, turning sharp left at Ling Hill Farm and later bearing right towards the coast and lighthouse. Just in front of the lighthouse gate, turn left over a stone stile to join the coast path **(D)**.

Follow the path along the top of the cliffs above Saltwick Bay, with some fine coastal scenery and spectacular views of the abbey ahead, for 2 miles (3.25 km) back to Whitby, climbing a succession of stiles and at one stage following a clearly marked route through a caravan site. On reaching a coastguard station **(E)**, continue past the abbey ruins on the left and take the paved path through the churchyard, passing the church on the right and continuing down the 199 steps to the harbour. At the bottom, turn left through the narrow streets of the old town back to the starting point.

31

8 Egton Bridge and the River Esk

Start:	Egton Bridge
Distance:	4 ½ miles (7.25 km)
Approximate time:	2 ½ hours
Parking:	By station in Egton Bridge
Refreshments:	Pubs in Egton Bridge
Ordnance Survey maps:	Landranger 94 (Whitby) and Outdoor Leisure 27 (North York Moors – Eastern area)

General description The River Esk is the only major river of the North York Moors, as well as being the only one that flows eastwards to the North Sea – all the others are little more than streams and flow southwards. This walk explores a particularly attractive section of the Esk valley between Egton Bridge and Glaisdale, its gentle and well-wooded scenery forming a striking contrast to much of the surrounding high, open moorland. Although a modest walk, there are three separate climbs and the last one, though short, is steep.

Walk along the road away from the railway bridge, following it as it bears right over the River Esk **(A)** through the small village of

Beggar's Bridge provides an attractive stop for walkers

32

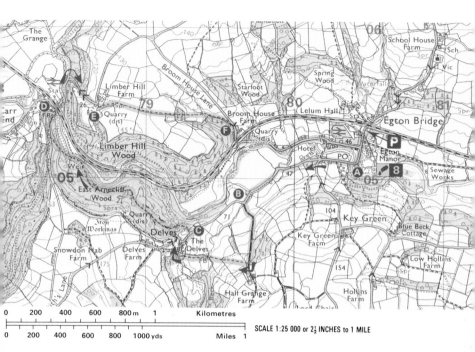

| 0 | 200 | 400 | 600 | 800 m | 1 | Kilometres |

| 0 | 200 | 400 | 600 | 800 | 1000 yds | Miles 1 |

SCALE 1:25 000 or 2½ INCHES to 1 MILE

Egton Bridge. At a junction, keep ahead along the lane signposted to Rosedale and Kirbymoorside, cross a footbridge beside a ford and continue by a stream on the left. Where the lane bends to the right, turn left, at a public bridleway sign **(B)**, over the stream and head uphill along a farm track, bearing right and passing the right-hand edge of a wood.

About 50 yards (46 m) before the track bears left to the farm, turn right over a stile, by a hedge-line on the right, and head downhill (no clear path), keeping close to the hedges on the right. Cross a beck in the bottom corner of the field, continue across rough pasture and, at the end of the next field, go through a gap in the hedge on the right and head straight across a field down to a footbridge. Cross over and continue uphill, (again no discernible path), keeping by a hedge and beck on the right, to the top of the field. Here climb a stone stile in the wall ahead and continue up to the top edge of the next field where you turn right and, with a glorious view to the right over the Esk valley, walk past The Delves Farm to a road. Turn right downhill for about 100 yards (92 m) and, at a footpath sign to Arncliff Woods, turn left along a broad track **(C)**. This partially paved track, once part of a pack-horse trail, continues through these most attractive woods, high above the river on the right, for 1 mile (1.5 km), at one stage passing a disused and now overgrown quarry and eventually descending to the riverbank to follow a particularly beautiful and tranquil

stretch of the Esk. Finally turn right down some steps to a footbridge over a stream by a ford, road and railway bridge **(D)**.

Cross the footbridge, continue under the railway bridge and ahead is Beggar's Bridge, an old, high-arched pack-horse bridge. Either cross that or the parallel road bridge over the Esk and continue along the road ahead, turning sharp right up the very steep Limber Hill. Where the road bends sharply to the left, turn right through a gate **(E)** at a public footpath sign and keep ahead a few yards (not on the track slightly to the right but along the grassy bank) to a gate on the left. Go through and keep along the edge of a field (by a hedge on the right), soon bearing right to join a wide track. Follow the track across the middle of a field to a stile. Climb over and, with lovely views down the Esk valley all the way, continue along the edge of the next field (by a hedge on the right) to a stile which admits you to a small plantation. Head steeply downhill through the plantation to another stile at the bottom end, climb that and continue downhill across the next field, bearing slightly left to a footbridge over a beck near the trees at the bottom. Cross the bridge, climb some steps opposite and continue along a path, by a wire fence and the edge of woodland on the right, to a stile.

Climb over, turn right down the road **(F)** and follow it for ¾ mile (1.25 km) into Egton Bridge, passing under a railway bridge and then keeping by the wooded banks of the Esk to a T-junction. Here turn left back to the starting point.

9 Ampleforth

Start:	Ampleforth
Distance:	4½ miles (7.25 km)
Approximate time:	2½ hours
Parking:	Village street in Ampleforth
Refreshments:	Pubs in Ampleforth
Ordnance Survey maps:	Landranger 100 (Malton & Pickering) and Outdoor Leisure 26 (North York Moors — Western area)

General description *From the pleasant old village of Ampleforth, nestling on the southern edge of the Moors, you climb steadily across breezy open countryside, passing an impressive prehistoric earthwork, before continuing along a lane and descending through the plantations of College Moor. The route back to Ampleforth gives glorious views across the Vale of York and the Howardian Hills to the south.*

Ampleforth is particularly noted for its abbey and college which lie about ½ mile (0.75 km) to the east. They were founded towards the end of the eighteenth century by Benedictine monks fleeing from the violence of the French Revolution. The village itself is most attractive, with a fine church and a main street lined with inns and stone cottages.

The walk, the first mile (1.5 km) of which is all uphill, begins in the main street between the White Horse and the post office, where there is a public footpath sign by the side of a telephone-box. Walk along a path between cottages and up the front drive of a house. Where the drive curves right up to the house, go through a gate on the left, turn right and head up to go through another gate. Continue up a steep grassy bank to yet another gate, go through that and keep ahead, by a house on the right, steeply uphill to join a path. Between fences on both sides, go through two more gates and keep ahead, by a fence on the right, to pass through another gate in the top corner of the field. Walk across the next field to a gate in its top right-hand corner, go through that and

Ampleforth village

34

continue, by a wall and wire fence on the right, to another gate. Pass through, turn left and then right to follow the edge of a field up to a metal gate. Now that you have almost completed the climb out of the village, there are fine open views all around.

Go through the gate and keep ahead, by a wire fence on the right, soon passing on the left the very obvious and most impressive Bronze Age stock enclosure of Studford Ring. Continue across the field in a straight line to a stile and footpath sign and climb over to join a lane (High Street) **(A)**. Turn left along it for just over ¾ mile (1.25 km) and, about 200 yards (184 m) past a turning to Ampleforth on the left, turn sharp left at a public footpath sign **(B)** and, after a few yards across rough scrub, turn left again to join a broad forest track which heads downhill through the pine woods of College Moor. Near the bottom of the hill bear left off the main track along a track through the trees; at first it runs roughly parallel to the previous track and then bears left away from it to a junction. Here it bends to the right but you take a narrow path that turns even more sharply right and heads through a wooded valley, descending quite steeply. Follow the direction indicated by a strategically placed

Ampleforth church

footpath sign to a stile a few yards ahead. Climb over and continue along a rough and not easily discernible path, between a stream on the right and a wire fence on the left, for a short distance to reach a broad track **(C)**.

Turn left, pass through a gate and continue along the track, from which there are fine views to the right over the valley to the Howardian Hills and later across the Vale of York. After a mile (1.5 km) you reach a road **(D)** where you turn left into Ampleforth.

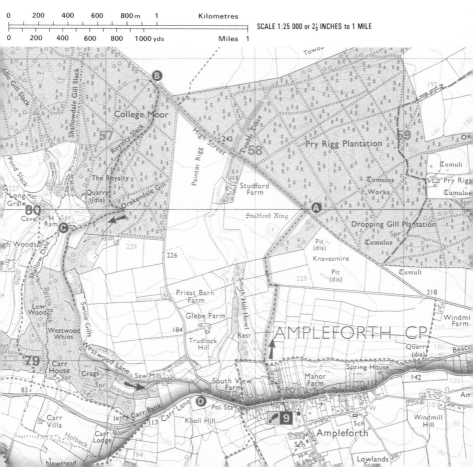

10 Hutton-le-Hole and Lastingham

Start:	Hutton-le-Hole
Distance:	6½ miles (10.5 km)
Approximate time:	3 hours
Parking:	Hutton-le-Hole
Refreshments:	Pubs and tea rooms at Hutton-le-Hole, pub at Lastingham
Ordnance Survey maps:	Landranger 94 (Whitby) and 100 (Malton & Pickering) and Outdoor Leisure 26 (North York Moors — Western area)

General description Two particularly attractive villages and a unique church are the chief features of interest on this relatively easy walk, mainly across fields, on the southern edge of the Moors, amidst the Tabular Hills. It is also a walk of scenic variety: bleak and open moorland to the north contrasting with the flatter and more lush landscape of the Vale of Pickering to the south.

With old stone houses and cottages scattered around a long, wide green which slopes down to a beck and is criss-crossed by paths and grazed by sheep, Hutton-le-Hole is one of the most popular, and is deservedly regarded as one of the most attractive, villages in North Yorkshire. People come here not just because of its beauty and fine location but also to visit the imaginative Ryedale Folk Museum, where a number of traditional buildings have been brought, rebuilt and restored to their original condition, housing various exhibits and examples of local crafts.

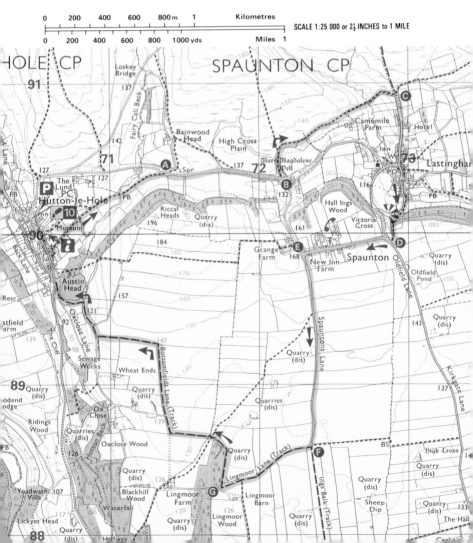

The magnificent Norman crypt at Lastingham

From the car park at the top end of the village, walk down the village street, past the tiny modern church and turn left through a gate at a public footpath sign. Follow the path round to the left to another gate, go through, turn right and head across a field by a fence on the left. Continue over two stiles, across the middle of a field to another stile, climb that and keep ahead across the next field to a gate and footbridge. Cross the bridge, continue through conifers to go through a gate and keep ahead along a pleasant grassy path, with fine views to the left over Spaunton Moor, to a road (A). Walk along it for ½ mile (0.75 km) — it has good wide verges — and, just before a bridge, turn left at a public footpath sign (B) along a path to a stile. Climb over and, with a fine view over bare moorland in front, keep ahead along a track which curves right along the edge of the moor, by a wall and fence on the right. Approaching a farm on the right, bear slightly left towards a wall corner (yellow waymark) and continue by a wall on the right, heading downhill. Cross a stream and continue straight up the hill on the other side to a wooden seat and footpath sign. Here turn right (C) down a broad track, through a gate and into the village of Lastingham.

The main claim to fame of this small and peaceful village is its fascinating church, on the site of an early Saxon monastery founded in the seventh century by St Cedd. In subsequent centuries the monastery suffered from Danish raids, but after the Norman Conquest Abbot Stephen of Whitby began the task of rebuilding it. This was never completed, however, in the thirteenth century the plans being abandoned and the monastery converted into a modest parish church which occupies the east end of the abbey. Fortunately much of Abbot Stephen's work remains — notably the superb apse at the east end (rare in English churches) and the unique aisled crypt, virtually unchanged since the eleventh century and a magnificent example of Norman architecture.

At a road junction make a brief detour to the right to visit the church; otherwise keep ahead and, where the road bends left, continue over a stream and along a tarmac lane by cottages. Where that lane becomes a rough track and starts to ascend, bear slightly right at a public footpath sign, along a grassy uphill path to a gate. Go through and continue through trees, climbing quite steeply. There are glorious views, to the right and behind, over Lastingham village, the church and the moors beyond. At the top, go through a gate by a footpath sign and continue to a junction of lanes (D). Keep ahead, following the lane to Spaunton, walk through the hamlet and, at a T-junction, turn left down a rough track (E).

Follow this track for ¾ mile (1.25 km) to a junction, turn right (F) along another broad track and keep along it towards a wood. On approaching the trees, bear right to a gate (G), go through, turn right and follow a path along the edge of the wood. After a while the path curves left and starts to head downhill, emerging from the wood and then ascending gently, lined with hedges, to a T-junction. Turn right and keep along a straight track, by a hedge on the left, for nearly ½ mile (0.75 km), following it round to the left and heading straight towards Hutton-le-Hole, which can be seen ahead. The track continues by bending right and descending between embankments to a gate. Go through and keep ahead, curving first left and then right to join a road. Turn right into the village.

11 Byland Abbey and Cockerdale

Start:	Byland Abbey
Distance:	6 miles (9.5 km)
Approximate time:	3 hours
Parking:	Roadside parking just to the south of Byland Abbey
Refreshments:	Pub at Byland Abbey
Ordnance Survey maps:	Landranger 100 (Malton & Pickering) and Outdoor Leisure 26 (North York Moors – Western area)

General description *Byland Abbey lies in a sheltered position amidst attractive and well wooded country on the southern fringes of the Moors. This varied and undemanding walk starts by heading across fields towards the hamlet of Wass, then climbs steadily through plantations onto the open expanses of Byland Moor. From there it descends through more woodland to Oldstead before returning across fields, with the west front of the abbey as a dominant landmark on this final leg.*

Although lacking the completeness of Rievaulx, the ruins of Byland Abbey are nevertheless interesting; Byland was the largest Cistercian monastery in England, its church being 330 feet (100 m) long. It was founded here in 1177, having moved from an earlier site at Old Byland because it was too close to Rievaulx – each monastery could hear the other's bells. The finest surviving

Ruined but still noble – the west front of Byland Abbey

portion is the ornate thirteenth-century west front. Most of the floor of the church was covered with glazed green and yellow geometrical tiles, and some of these survive in two chapels in the south transept.

Start by the west front of the abbey (opposite the Abbey Inn) and walk along the road signposted to Wass, Ampleforth and Helmsley. Turn left at a public footpath sign **(A)** along the drive leading towards Abbey House and, just before reaching the buildings, turn right through a gate (yellow waymark) and head along the side of a field to another gate. Go through that and continue, bearing left slightly uphill towards the top corner of the field below a wooded embankment. Here climb a fence and continue to a metal gate. Go through and keep ahead, with the houses of the hamlet of Wass on the right, to go through another metal gate at a public footpath sign **(B)**.

Turn left along a narrow uphill lane which, after passing through another gate, soon becomes a rough woodland track. Continue through the attractive Abbey Bank Wood and, where the track forks, climb the stile ahead at a footpath sign to continue along a path that bisects the two forks, initially by the edge of woods with a wire fence on the left. On approaching a group of trees ahead, bear right to take a slightly uphill path through those trees, keeping in a straight line and making for a stile in front. Climb over and you are confronted with two tracks ahead. Take the left-hand one through the dense conifers of Snever Wood, climbing steadily until you emerge from the trees at a gate and yellow waymark.

Go through and continue along the edge of the field in front, by a wall on the left, over the open country of Byland Moor with fine views all around. Go through a gate, keep ahead to go through another one and continue in a straight line for about 200 yards (184 m) before turning left and heading straight across the field towards the far left-hand corner of the buildings of Cam Farm. Here go through a gate with a yellow waymark, keep ahead through another gate and continue towards the house just ahead. Bear left, walk between the house and a barn and keep ahead, at a yellow arrow, to a gate. Go through and, with fine views of wooded Cockerdale below on the left, follow a downhill track, passing through a gate and into woodland. Take the first turning on the left **(C)**, a sharp bend, along a track which soon curves right and continues downhill for ¾ mile (1.25 km) through Great Cockerdale Wood, eventually passing through a gate into more open country.

Keep along the still-curving downhill track, turning left at a T-junction. About 100 yards (92 m) ahead **(D)**, bear left along a lane and

SCALE 1:25 000 or 2½ INCHES to 1 MILE

shortly afterwards turn left, at a public footpath sign, along a track by the side of a house. Follow this track through an avenue of trees towards Oldstead Hall and, just before reaching the hall, turn right by a wooden fence on the right and scramble up a steep embankment to a stile. Climb over and continue along the top edge of a wood on the left, climbing three stiles before reaching a lane (E). Turn sharp right and, just where the lane bends to the right, turn left at a public footpath sign along a farm track to Oldstead Grange. Follow the track through a farmyard, pass through a metal gate at the far end and head across the middle of a field to the bottom corner. Here bear right through a metal gate and then bear left uphill along a narrow path, between trees and bushes, to a footpath sign to Byland Abbey. Continue along the edge of a field, by a hedge on the left, with pleasant views of rolling country

ahead, following the field boundary round to the left to a stile and footpath sign.

Climb over, continue along the left-hand edge of a field and now for the first time there are attractive glimpses in front of the abbey ruins. At the bottom end of the next field, bear left through a gap and then immediately right (at a Byland Abbey footpath sign) to follow the right-hand edge of the next field. Climb a stile, continue along the edge of a field to climb another one and then bear slightly left, across the middle of the next field, to a stile by a solitary tree. Climb over and continue across a field to a gate in a fence on the left. From here there is a splendid view of the west front of the abbey. Do not go through the gate but keep ahead, by the fence on the left, to a stile. Climb over, turn left along the road back to the abbey, and over to the left, as an extra bonus, there is a good view of the White Horse of Kilburn.

12 Bransdale and Rudland Rigg

Start:	Cockayne
Distance:	6 miles (9.5 km)
Approximate time:	3 hours
Parking:	By road just below Cockayne church
Refreshments:	None
Ordnance Survey maps:	Landranger 94 (Whitby) and 100 (Malton & Pickering) and Outdoor Leisure 26 (North York Moors – Western area)

General description *Solitude and wild beauty are the main features of this walk in an area that could scarcely be more remote, linked to the 'outside world' by just one narrow lane. From the head of Bransdale you climb up onto Rudland Rigg to follow an old coach road over open moorland, from which there are glorious and expansive views in all directions, before dropping back into the dale and returning across fields to the starting point.*

St Nicholas's Church and the scattering of houses at the head of Bransdale make up the isolated hamlet of Cockayne. The tiny, plain church matches its surroundings perfectly and faces southwards down the dale, sheltered by Rudland Rigg to the east, Bilsdale East Moor to the west and the forested slopes of Bransdale Moor to the north.

Start by walking along the narrow winding lane for ½ mile (0.75 km) in the Kirbymoorside direction, crossing a stream and turning left over a stile at the first public bridle-way sign **(A)**. Follow a sunken path uphill and go through a gap in a wall, heading towards the edge of a plantation from where the views down Bransdale are superb. Continue along the curving path to the edge of the trees, bear right along them and then bear left towards the corner of the plantation, going through a metal gate. Keep ahead by the trees for a few yards and then follow the path that bears right, heading uphill across rough open moorland. The path curves gently to the right through the heather to join a broad, straight, sandy track **(B)**, once an old high-level coach road across the moors between Stokesley and Kirbymoorside.

Turn right along this track, which heads across wild, open heather moorland between

The church at Cockayne sits snugly at the head of Bransdale

Bransdale on the right and Farndale on the left, ascending Rudland Rigg, as far as a crossroads of tracks **(C)**. Here turn right along another track, cross a stream and head up to Shaw Ridge ahead. On reaching the ridge, turn left onto a broad track **(D)** which heads southwards along it for just under a mile (1.5 km), descending to a lane **(E)**.

Turn sharp right along this winding lane for ¾ mile (1.25 km) and, as it descends into Bransdale, there is a superb view ahead looking towards the head of the dale with Bransdale Lodge and Cockayne church clearly visible. Soon after passing a cattle-grid, take a sharp left turn through Spout House Farm and, just past the farm buildings, turn right **(F)** along the edge of a field, by a wall on the left, down to a gate. Go through and now follow a clearly waymarked route through a succession of gates, eventually dropping down to cross a stream just in front of a gate. Go through that gate and continue above Hodge Beck on the left, passing the top edge of the trees that clothe the side of the beck. Pass through two more gates and continue through trees to the buildings of Bransdale Mill. There has been a mill on this site since the Middle Ages but the present buildings date from the nineteenth century when the mill was expanded by William Strickland. It is now owned by the National Trust and has been recently restored.

Turn right in front of the mill and ascend some stone steps to climb a ladder stile. Continue in a straight line, by a wall on the right, climb a ladder stile in that wall and turn left along the edge of a field, by a hedge and wire fence on the left, to climb another ladder stile ahead. Continue to Cow Sike Farm, go through a gate and on through the farmyard to a lane. Turn left and follow the lane for nearly ¾ mile (1.25 km) back to Cockayne.

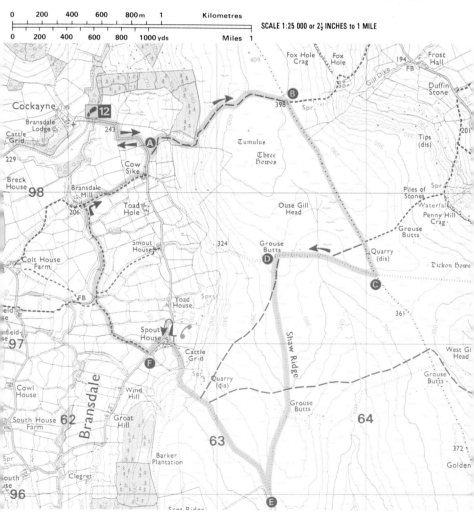

SCALE 1:25 000 or 2½ INCHES to 1 MILE

13 Hole of Horcum

Start:	Car park on A169 above Hole of Horcum about ½ mile (0.75 km) south of Saltergate Inn
Distance:	7 miles (11.25 km)
Approximate time:	3½ hours
Parking:	Hole of Horcum
Refreshments:	Pub at Levisham
Ordnance Survey maps:	Landranger 94 (Whitby) and 100 (Malton & Pickering) and Outdoor Leisure 27 (North York Moors — Eastern area)

General description *The walk begins from a fine vantage point above the great natural amphitheatre of the Hole of Horcum and follows moorland tracks along its rim to the village of Levisham. From there it descends through woodland and returns along the valley of Levisham Beck below the rim. The views are spectacular all the way and the only steep climb comes right at the end in order to get back onto the top edge of the 'Hole'*

From the car park there is an outstanding view ahead over the Hole of Horcum, the first of many on this walk. Although ancient local folk-tales attribute its creation to a giant who scooped out the 'Hole' to make his home in it, the dramatic, steep, smooth-sided ravine was formed as a result of erosion by escaping torrents of melt-water from the great ice-blocked lake which filled Esk Dale towards the end of the Ice Age.

Turn right and walk along the main road in the Whitby direction, following it as it curves to the left and, at a sharp right-hand bend **(A)**, keep ahead to an adjacent gate and stile. Go through the gate and continue along a broad grassy track, from where there are fine views to the right over Lockton High Moor and Fylingdales Moor. The track heads across heathery moorland above the Hole of Horcum, curving gradually to the left all the while. It passes two ponds on the right — an unusual feature on these well-drained moors. The first is Seavy Pond, after which the track crosses an Iron Age dyke and continues to Dundale Pond **(B)**. A stone in the ground indicates that this was probably made in the thirteenth century by the monks of Malton Priory, who owned the land and used it as pasture for their sheep, cattle and horses. Dundale Pond is a meeting place of tracks and here you bear slightly right uphill to a stile. Climb over **(C)** and continue along the broad, walled track ahead, which later joins a lane and descends into Levisham — a remote, pretty, one-street village with a wide green lined with cottages and a pub.

At the bottom end of the village, turn left at a footpath sign with a white arrow **(D)**, beside a bench, along a path that heads down through trees and bushes above the steep-sided valley on the right. After descending, the path then climbs some steps and follows the side of the valley round to the left, descending again through woodland and continuing above Levisham Beck. Eventually the path emerges from the trees and drops down, through a gate, to join the beck at a crossroads of paths.

Cross a tributary beck, then cross Levisham Beck by a footbridge a few yards

Approaching the great natural amphitheatre of the 'Hole of Horcum'

ahead and bear slightly left, between the beck on the left and a wall on the right, to a stile. Climb over, keep ahead to climb another one and continue by a wire fence on the right. Where that fence ends, follow the direction of a yellow waymark straight across the middle of a field, with woods on the right and the beck on the left, to Low Horcum

Farm. Keep to the left of the farm and continue along a path which heads across grass to a gate and stile. Climb the stile to commence the ascent, through rough grass, bracken and heather, up the side of the Hole of Horcum to a ladder stile at the top edge. Climb that, continue a few yards to the road and bear right back to the car park.

14 Newton Dale and Levisham

Start:	Newton-on-Rawcliffe
Distance:	6 miles (9.5 km)
Approximate time:	3 hours
Parking:	Along village streets in Newton-on-Rawcliffe
Refreshments:	Pub at Newton-on-Rawcliffe, pub at Levisham
Ordnance Survey maps:	Landranger 94 (Whitby) and 100 (Malton & Pickering) and Outdoor Leisure 27 (North York Moors – Eastern area)

General description *The narrow, steep-sided and thickly-wooded Newton Dale was carved out by melt-water from glaciers during the Ice Age. Rather more recently Victorian railway engineers saw it as a good route and constructed a line through it linking Pickering with Grosmont and Whitby. Although the line was axed in the 1960s, walkers can still on large parts of this route see and hear the sounds of steam engines as the line has now been restored as the North York Moors Railway. The walk includes two typical Moors villages, passes through some fine wooded stretches and involves two modest climbs.*

Newton-on-Rawcliffe is a quiet remote moorland village with a pond and one street lined with wide greens – similar to Levisham, passed through later on the walk. Begin by going through a gate on the right-hand side of the White Swan and walk along

a path, passing through two more gates in quick succession and continuing across a narrow field to a gate and stile. Climb over, continue across another narrow field to climb another stile, turn right for a few yards and, at a public bridle-way sign, turn sharp left **(A)** along a track that heads down the wooded Newton Banks.

As you descend there are fine views over the thickly-wooded slopes of Newton Dale. Climb a stile and bear right across a field, heading in the direction of the railway line. The path is not very clear at this point but continue between gorse bushes, bear right through a group of trees and on down to a footbridge over a stream. Cross it and continue over the level-crossing by Levisham station, a popular stopping place on the North Yorkshire Moors Railway. The line between Pickering and Whitby was constructed by the 'father of the railways', George Stephenson, and opened in 1836. On this section of it his major problem was the boggy terrain of the dale, which he overcame by laying down a foundation which comprised a mixture of heather and sheep hides. Since being restored as a mainly steam-operated railway, it has become a major tourist attraction.

Continue past the railway to a public footpath sign, where you turn right **(B)** through a gate along a most attractive, wooded uphill path to a gate at the top edge of the woods. Go through and continue along the side of a field, by a wire fence on the left, following the field boundary as it curves right to a stile just to the left of a gate. Climb the stile, turn right and, after a few yards, bear left along a grassy uphill path heading away from the wire fence on the right. From this point the views across the dale are superb, but although the steam

Steam trains still run through wooded Newton Dale

SCALE 1:25 000 or 2½ INCHES to 1 MILE

trains can be frequently heard, they can be only occasionally glimpsed because of the dense woodlands that line the sides of the dale. The path curves left in front of a well-placed wooden seat, continues along the side of a steep bank and then turns right along the top edge of a wood, heading up to a stile. Climb it, climb another one a few yards ahead and continue along the edge of a field, by a wall on the left, with extensive views to the right of the Tabular Hills and beyond them the Vale of Pickering and the Wolds. Climb a stile, continue along the edge of a field to climb another one and follow a lane into the small village of Levisham (C), turning right down the village street which, like that of Newton-on-Rawcliffe, is bordered by wide greens and lined with cottages.

At the bottom end of the village, continue along the road which curves first right and then sharp left downhill and, at a public bridle-way sign, turn right (D) along a track that keeps along the bottom edge of the steep-sided Row Wood to the right. Soon you turn left along a grassy path that heads down past Levisham's medieval church, beautifully situated in a bowl of wooded hills but now disused and sadly falling into ruin, passing to the left of the church and continuing to a footbridge. Cross over, turn right by a stream for a few yards and continue through a gate and along an uphill path, bordered by a wire fence on the right and trees and hedges on the left, curving left to join a broad track. Here turn right, pass through a gate and walk along this pleasantly tree-lined track for 1 mile (1.5 km), keeping roughly parallel with the stream, whose sparkling waters can be seen at times below on the right. Eventually you reach a gate at

0 200 400 600 800 m 1 Kilometre
0 200 400 600 800 1000 yds

the far end of the woods. Go through it, keep ahead for about 200 yards (184 m) and bear right through another gate.

Cross the railway line, by the old, isolated, railwaymen's cottages at Farwath (E), bear right over a footbridge and continue along a broad track, shortly bearing right at a fork along a much narrower but still clear track. Follow this through woodland and across rough grassland for 1½ miles (2.5 km), keeping parallel with the railway line on the right. On reaching a gate go through it, continue through three more gates, keep ahead for about 100 yards (92 m) and then turn left (F), heading uphill across the field towards the woods ahead. Bear right on reaching the edge of the trees and where the path meets a wire fence on the left, climb over (no stile), turn left and head steeply uphill through the trees, bending sharply to the right and later curving left to reach a stile. Climb it to join the outward route (A) and retrace your steps to Newton-on-Rawcliffe.

45

15 Ainthorpe Rigg and Little Fryup Dale

Start:	National Park Information Centre at Danby Lodge
Distance:	6 miles (9.5 km)
Approximate time:	3 hours
Parking:	Danby Lodge
Refreshments:	Café at Danby Lodge, pub at Ainthorpe
Ordnance Survey maps:	Landranger 94 (Whitby) and Outdoor Leisure 27 (North York Moors — Eastern area)

General description *Lush green pastures by the River Esk at the start, followed by a steady climb across heathery moorland onto Ainthorpe Rigg and a descent into the beautiful, thinly-populated Little Fryup Dale, make this a particularly attractive and absorbing walk with constantly outstanding views. Castle ruins and a picturesque pack-horse bridge add to the variety and enjoyment, and the well-stocked National Park Information Centre at Danby Lodge makes an excellent starting and finishing point.*

From the car park cross the road, go through a gate at a public footpath sign, and walk across a field by a wire fence on the right, with Danby Lodge over to the right. Cross

SCALE 1:25 000 or 2½ INCHES to 1 MILE

Little Fryup Dale lies below Ainthorpe Rigg

the footbridge over the River Esk and continue along a well-waymarked path, keeping by a fence and hedge on the right, to the railway line. Cross that and keep ahead, with fine views all around of the river valley, rolling wooded hills and, beyond them, glimpses of moorland.

Head towards a stile in the far left-hand corner of the field, climb over and turn right along a narrow lane (A). At the first public footpath sign on the left, climb a stile and walk along the edge of a field, between a wire fence on the right and hedge on the left, following it round to the right to climb another stile. From here there is a good view of Danby village to the right. Continue along the edge of the next field, this time with a wall on the right, to go through a gate. Bear slightly left along the edge of the next field, by a wall on the left, climb a stile and continue along a walled track into Ainthorpe. Go through a gate and turn left along a lane (B), immediately passing the Fox and Hounds on the left, and continue along it for ¼ mile (0.5 km).

Where the lane bends left, just past Danby Tennis Club, bear slightly right, at a public bridle-way sign, along a grassy path which heads across open moorland between gorse, bracken and heather, continuing through a gate and climbing towards the ridge in front. The path is easy to follow, lined with cairns, and the contrast between the wildness of the moor and the earlier lushness by the river near Danby Lodge is very striking. Keep in a fairly straight line over Ainthorpe Rigg, after which the path descends into Little Fryup Dale with a magnificent view of the dale in front, Great Fryup Dale beyond and Danby Rigg curving round to the right.

Drop down to a road junction (C) and walk along the lane directly opposite, with the distinctive Round Hill ahead acting as a kind of sentinel guarding Great Fryup Dale. Follow the lane into the dale bottom, passing a farm and some cottages and, after climbing gently for a few yards, turn left through a metal gate (D) past the prominent buildings of Stonebeck Gate Farm on the left. Continue in front of the farmhouse and along a broad, fairly straight, walled track, from which there are the most superb views ahead down Little Fryup Dale to Eskdale. Go through three metal gates in turn and then turn left down another walled track towards a farm. Turn right through a gate just in front of the farm and bear left to skirt the corner of the farm buildings, heading diagonally across a field down to a gate and yellow waymark. Go through, keep ahead a few yards to go through another gate and continue along a reasonably clear, grassy path which soon curves left over a footbridge. Now follow a track which heads uphill, passing through a gate and continuing for a short distance across open moorland up to a lane (E).

Turn right along this lane for just over ½ mile (0.75 km) to the scanty but nevertheless impressive remains of Danby Castle, adjacent to a farm. This fourteenth-century structure, more of a domestic building than a fortress, was once the administrative centre of the region. At the junction of lanes by the castle, bear right to continue down a narrow lane to Duck Bridge (F), one of a number of picturesque pack-horse bridges over the Esk. Do not turn right over the bridge but keep along the lane ahead for another ½ mile (0.75 km) and, soon after crossing a beck, turn right over a stile, at a public footpath sign, and retrace your steps over the railway and river to Danby Lodge.

16 Rosedale Abbey and the ironstone railway

Start:	Rosedale Abbey
Distance:	7 miles (11.25 km)
Approximate time:	3½ hours
Parking:	Rosedale Abbey
Refreshments:	Pubs and cafés at Rosedale Abbey
Ordnance Survey maps:	Landranger 94 (Whitby) and 100 (Malton & Pickering), Outdoor Leisure 26 (North York Moors – Western area)

General description *When walking through Rosedale today it is difficult to imagine that this lovely, peaceful valley, surrounded by empty moorland, was once a busy iron-mining area that fuelled the industries of Teesside. The mining of iron ore, initiated in the area in the Middle Ages by the nuns of the priory at Rosedale, reached its climax in the nineteenth century when the population of the dale soared to nearly 3,000 and a railway was built to carry the ore across the bleak moors to Bloworth Crossing, from where it was lowered down Greenhow Bank to the plain below and then on to the furnaces of Middlesbrough. Vestiges of this industry still remain – old mine workings, ruins of mine buildings, iron-workers' cottages and, above all, the route of the ironstone railway itself which forms nearly half of this walk. It is an outstandingly attractive and interesting walk – the gentle scenery of the dale contrasting with the rugged terrain of the encircling moors, and the railway and other reminders of Rosedale's industrial past contrasting even more strongly with its present rural tranquillity.*

Rosedale is illustrated on the front cover.

Please note that the part of the Rosedale Ironstone Railway used on this walk is not a public right of way, but the owners permit walkers to use it provided that the Country Code is adhered to and all dogs are kept on leads.

Since the closure of the iron mines and railway, Rosedale Abbey has lapsed again into being a sparsely-populated backwater and now its principal industry is tourism. Of the twelfth-century abbey – strictly speaking a priory of Cistercian nuns – virtually nothing remains except for a small turret by the church.

Start by turning left out of the car park and then immediately right, across the village green, turning right again between houses along a tarmac lane that passes the front of the church and the meagre ruins of the priory. On the left are two public footpath signs; climb a stone stile by the far one and, in a few yards, bear right along a track through a caravan site. At a footpath sign, bear slightly right to go through a metal gate and continue along the edge of a field, by a hedge and wire fence bordering the caravan site on the left. Climb a stile, continue along a path that gently descends towards the little River Seven on the left and climb another stile to enter a small wood. Keep ahead, ignoring the footbridge on the left, and, at a fork, take the left-hand path, by the river and wooden fence on the left, down to a stile. Climb over and, following yellow waymarks, continue across two fields, over a ladder stile and, with grand views all the way up Rosedale, keep ahead across the middle of the next field to climb another stile. Bear left along a track, which descends to cross a minor stream and then continues beside the River Seven to a footbridge (**A**).

Do not cross the footbridge on the left but bear right and follow a clear, paved path across the middle of the field to a stile in a

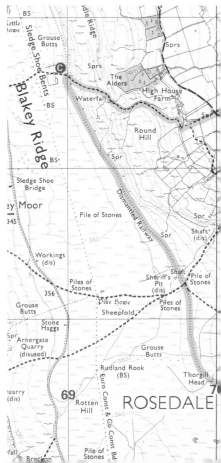

SCALE 1:25 000 or 2½ INCHES to 1 MILE

hedge. Climb over and, bearing slightly right, continue up to a gap in the hedge in front; go through and keep ahead uphill to pass through a gate. Bear left along a path between hedge-banks, continuing to Hill Cottages in front and eventually curving left and right to join a lane (**B**).

Turn left, walk past the Ebenezer Methodist Church and, just past the Rosedale East Post Office, turn left at a public footpath sign down a tarmac farm lane, between cottages and houses, to a metal gate. Go through, keep ahead through a farmyard, passing through another gate, and continue along the edge of a field, by a wooden fence on the right, down to a gate. Over to the right is an impressive view of old mine workings. Go through the gate and continue, now by a hedge and later a fence on the right, to pass through another gate and descend by a stream on the right, continuing across the next field and then bearing left to go through yet another gate. Cross a farm track, go through the gate opposite, at a footpath sign, and continue along the edge of a field, by a wire fence on the right, to go through a metal gate. Now bear slightly left away from the fence to a marker post and continue past it to a gate.

Do not go through it but turn right, over a ladder stile a few yards in front. Keep ahead for about 50 yards (46 m) to another marker post and turn left along an uphill path across rough open grassland. The path passes close to the edge of a plantation on the right and continues winding upwards. There is no clear path in places but simply make your way to the top of the ridge ahead where, after quite a steep climb, you turn left along a broad flat track (**C**).

This is the bed of the former Rosedale Ironstone Railway and you keep along this superb high-level route for nearly 3 miles (4.75 km), passing abandoned mine workings and with outstanding views all the way over Rosedale to the left and across wide expanses of open moorland ahead and to the right. There is a particularly impressive view where the track curves left above a steep wooded bank, with the village of Rosedale Abbey below and the 'golf balls' of Fylingdales early warning station on the horizon.

Above the village and just before the track bears right by a large house, bear left at a fork (**D**), by a small pile of stones, and head towards the house. About 100 yards (92 m) in front of it, turn left off the track along a broad grassy path which heads downhill and curves left to a stile. Climb over and continue downhill, by a wire fence and broken wall on the right, curving right and heading steeply down to a ladder stile in that wall. Climb it, continue to another ladder stile in a wall on the right, climb that and keep ahead along a clearly marked footpath across part of a golf-course. Turn left in front of wooden buildings down to a stile, climb it, cross the lane to climb another stile by a public footpath sign opposite and continue along the edge of a field, by a hedge on the right, towards the village. Climb a stile, go down steps by the side of a house, continue through a gate and along the lane ahead to a T-junction and on into Rosedale Abbey.

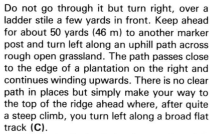

17 Guisborough and Highcliffe Nab

Start:	Guisborough
Distance:	7 miles (11.25 km)
Approximate time:	3 ½ hours
Parking:	Guisborough
Refreshments:	Pubs and cafés at Guisborough
Ordnance Survey maps:	Landranger 94 (Whitby) and Outdoor Leisure 26 (North York Moors — Western area)

The east front is the chief surviving remnant of Guisborough Priory

General description *This is an 'up, across and down' walk. From the centre of Guisborough, you quickly emerge into open country and proceed across fields to the base of the Cleveland escarpment. A relatively modest climb up to the top is followed by a pleasant and easy ramble through conifer woods to the superb vantage point of Highcliffe Nab. Finally you descend from the escarpment through more woodland for the return across fields to Guisborough.*

Guisborough, the ancient capital of Cleveland, has grown rapidly over the last twenty to thirty years and its sprawling residential estates can be seen from the higher points on this walk. The walk also reveals the obvious reason for this growth: its

ideal position for commuters — within easy reach of, but away from, the industries of Teesside and pleasantly situated amidst attractive countryside, at the foot of the Cleveland Hills, on the fringe of the moors and within easy reach of the coast. The once large and powerful Augustinian priory, founded in the early twelfth century by Robert de Brus, ancestor of the famous

Scottish king, and dissolved in 1539, comprises little more than the east end of the church. But what a magnificent fragment that is: standing to its full height, virtually complete and regarded as a masterpiece of Decorated architecture.

Start in the main street by walking along the A171 in the Whitby direction. Where that road turns right, continue towards the late medieval church and walk along the paved path by the left-hand side of the church. At the end of the churchyard, bear right through a kissing-gate and follow a path across the field ahead, passing the ruins of Guisborough Priory on the right. Beyond the ruins is a good view of the wooded escarpment of the Cleveland Hills. Pass through another kissing-gate and continue through a small group of trees to a third kissing-gate and onto the main road. Turn left for about 100 yards (92 m) and, at a public footpath sign, turn right **(A)** along a broad track to Foxdale Farm. Where the track bears right, look out for a stile and public footpath sign in a fence on the left. Climb over and walk along the edge of a field, by a wooden fence on the right, go through a kissing-gate and keep straight ahead, this time with a wire fence on

the left, ascending gently all the while. Climb a stile and continue along a narrow, hedge-lined path, from which there are lovely views all around of gentle, rolling, wooded hills and fields dotted with farmhouses. The path drops down to a stile; climb it, keep along the edge of the next field to climb another stile and continue over a further stile to rejoin the main road **(B)**.

Here turn right immediately along the track signposted to Old Park Farm, passing Little Waterfall Farm on the right, and continue over a disused railway line and along the edge of a field, by a hedge on the left. At a fork, take the left-hand track which proceeds upwards towards the top of the wooded escarpment ahead. On reaching the trees you join the Cleveland Way, continuing uphill along a concrete farm road.

At the point where you leave the trees, go through a metal gate and turn right **(C)** over a stile and across a field. From here there is an extensive view to the right over Guisborough and beyond the town to the coast and industries of Teesside. A grassy path leads you to the edge of woodland where you go through a gate with a Cleveland Way sign on the right and then turn left to follow a path along the edge of the trees. The views from this path — to the right over Guisborough and the coast and to the left across Gisborough Moor — are superb; but they are the last for a while for soon the track bears left into the dense conifer plantations of Guisborough Woods and continues through them for the next 2 miles (3.25 km), eventually reaching the notable viewpoint of Highcliffe Nab. From this bird's eye position there is a magnificent panorama over the town, coast, moors and thickly-wooded slopes of the Cleveland Hills.

From the Nab, head steeply downhill to a yellow marker post, turn left through conifers and drop down to a broad track. Turn right along this track, and, at a T-junction, turn right again **(D)** along a forestry road, following it for ¾ mile (1.25 km). After a descent, turn left along a broad track, just before the road starts to ascend, down to the edge of the woods where you turn right **(E)** along a path that heads initially through the trees towards farm buildings and then keeps along the edge of the trees by a wire fence on the left.

Climb a stile and continue over the shoulder of a modest hill, between bushes of gorse and broom, and cross a large open field, parallel to the edge of the trees on the right and houses of Guisborough on the left. On reaching a gate, go through, turn left **(F)** along a hedge-lined path which later becomes a tarmac lane and continue along it for just over ¾ mile (1.25 km) back to the town centre.

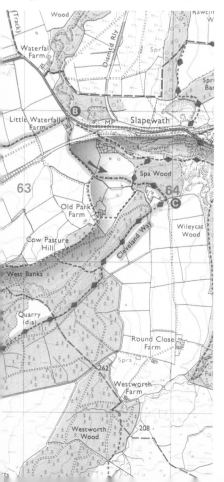

18 Black Hambleton

Start:	Right-angled bend on minor road from Osmotherley to Hawnby, about 2½ miles (4 km) south-west of Osmotherley
Distance:	7½ miles (12 km)
Approximate time:	4 hours
Parking:	Large parking area at bend in road
Refreshments:	None
Ordnance Survey maps:	Landranger 100 (Malton & Pickering) and Outdoor Leisure 26 (North York Moors — Western area)

General description *Black Hambleton is the brooding, whale-backed hill that dominates the skyline of the Hambleton Hills, especially when seen from the Vale of Mowbray to the west. The walk starts from just below the hill, descends through the conifer plantations of Cleveland Forest and continues across farmland below the escarpment, before climbing on to it. The finale is a glorious 3-mile (4.75-km) ramble along the Hambleton Drove Road, over the shoulder of Black Hambleton, from which the views are magnificent.*

Start by walking southwards along the wide track, part of the Hambleton Drove Road, towards Black Hambleton, the prominent hill directly ahead. Climb a stile and continue to the edge of the conifer plantations. Here turn right through a gate **(A)**, at a bridle-way sign to Nether Silton, along a path through the trees, bearing left on joining a forest road. Follow this road for just over 1 mile (1.5 km), heading downhill and then slightly up again to the Silton picnic area. Past there the road leaves the forest and continues towards a farm.

Just after crossing a stream, turn left through a metal gate **(B)** and walk straight across the field ahead to another metal gate. Go through that and, with a fine view of Black Hambleton to the left, walk across the next field to a stile and yellow waymark. Climb over and bear right in the direction of the waymark, heading diagonally across the

next field to a metal gate and another yellow waymark. Go through and keep along the edge of a field, by a wire fence and hedge on the left. In front are superb views of the Hambleton Hills and the Vale of York beyond. At the end of the field follow a waymark to the right, shortly afterwards turning left over a stile and continuing along the left-hand edge of the next field down to a stile in its bottom corner. Climb over, cross a track, climb another stile almost opposite and continue along the edge of the next field by a hedge on the left. Pass through two gates, cross a footbridge over a ditch and head straight across a field to go through a gate onto a narrow lane **(C)**. Turn left for about ½ mile (0.75 km) and, where the lane bends sharply to the right **(D)**, continue ahead along an uphill track past Nab Farm, drawing closer to the Hambleton Hills. Keep to the right of the farm buildings, pass through two gates and continue along a path which, after a while, bears right and heads down to cross a stream. The path then bears left to ascend to a gate by an old limekiln. Go through and climb steadily between rough grass, bracken and heather, joining a wall on the right and keeping by it to the top of the escarpment.

Here go through a gate and turn left **(E)** along a wide, grassy, walled track. This is the Hambleton Drove Road, a particularly impressive example of a number of such routes across the country, along which cattle and sheep were driven from their pastures in Scotland, Wales and elsewhere to the growing markets in the Midlands and south of England during the early days of the Industrial Revolution, before the railways made them obsolete. Follow the drove road through several gates back to the starting point, a superb high-level moorland walk of nearly 3 miles (4.75 km) with magnificent views all the way across the broad Vales of York and Mowbray to the line of the Pennines. The route is easy to follow, keeping by a wall on the left all the way and turning left at a marker-post to head over the shoulder of Black Hambleton. As you descend towards the starting point the views change: ahead, in the foreground, is the village of Osmotherley and beyond that the Cleveland Plain stretching away in the distance to County Durham; to the right the Cleveland Hills and to the left the dense plantations of Cleveland Forest with, as always, the Pennines on the western horizon.

SCALE 1:25 000 or 2½ INCHES to 1 MILE

```
0     200   400   600   800 m    1        Kilometres
|-----|-----|-----|-----|-----|-----|
0     200   400   600   800  1000 yds    Miles      1
```

19 Runswick Bay and Staithes

Ordnance Survey maps: Landranger 94 (Whitby) and Outdoor Leisure 27 (North York Moors — Eastern area)

Start:	Runswick Bay
Distance:	7½ miles (12 km)
Approximate time:	4 hours
Parking:	Runswick Bay
Refreshments:	Pubs and cafés at Runswick Bay, Fox and Hounds just before Staithes, pubs and cafés at Staithes

General description In very different ways, both Runswick Bay and Staithes are highly individual coastal villages: the former a picturesque jumble of cottages above a fine sandy beach, the latter an old harbour, still with a strong Victorian atmosphere, beside a steep-sided inlet. The first half of the walk from Runswick Bay to Staithes goes inland, following an attractive route across fields, by

SCALE 1:25 000 or 2½ INCHES to 1 MILE

farms and through woodlands. The return journey is along a memorable stretch of the North Sea coast where, as on most coastal paths, there are a number of ascents and descents.

Runswick Bay is one of the most attractive villages on the North Yorkshire coast and a paradise for artists and photographers. Its cottages perch randomly and almost precariously on a series of terraces on the hillside above the beach and there are no streets but narrow passageways and flights of steps that open up new vistas all the time as they twist and turn between the buildings.

Start at the bottom car park just above the beach (there is another car park at the top of the village that could be used as an alternative starting point) and walk up the steep road to Runswick Bank Top. Turn half-left along Hinderwell Lane and, after just over ¼ mile (0.5 km), turn left **(A)** over a stile, at a public footpath sign, and walk along the edge of a field, by a hedge on the left. Climb another stile and continue along the edge of the next field, following it round to the right to climb a stile, at a public footpath sign, onto the main road. Turn right for 100 yards (92 m) and take the first turning on the left **(B)** to follow a narrow lane for nearly 1 mile (1.5 km) into Newton Mulgrave. After passing through the hamlet, turn right through a gate **(C)**, at the second public footpath sign, along a broad track.

Follow the track through one gate, do not go through a second gate but keep to the left of it, along the right-hand edge of the field, to pass through another gate. Continue along the edge of the next field, by the top edge of a wood on the left (the path is narrow at this point and can sometimes be overgrown), and

look out for a path junction near a view of the houses of Hinderwell over to the right. At this point, do not turn left along the obvious path down through the woods but bear slightly left along another woodland path, keeping roughly in the same direction as before, and follow it as it winds through this very attractive woodland, keeping roughly half-way between the top of the wooded bank on the right and a stream on the left. Climb a stile to emerge from the wood, continue along a grassy ledge (the view ahead now dominated by Boulby potash mine), climb another stile and descend between hedges over a third stile. Cross a bridge a little further on and continue along a track, by the stream on the left, to reach a lane **(D)**. Turn right, passing the Fox and Hounds on the left, and climb quite steeply up to the main road.

Turn right and then take the first turning on the left **(E)** to walk through the upper, modern part of Staithes, before descending steeply through the old fishing village down to the harbour. Lack of space on the side of this deep, steep-sided, narrow inlet is responsible for the tall, tightly-packed buildings and narrow streets leading down to the small, but very atmospheric harbour. In his youth Captain Cook was apprenticed to a draper here but the shop in which he worked, like many of Staithes' old buildings throughout the centuries, has been swept away by ferocious North Sea storms. The pub has been rebuilt several times, the last occasion being in 1953.

At the harbour turn right **(F)** up Church Street, passing the Mission Church on the right, climbing steeply to the top. Keep ahead up some steps and turn left, at a Cleveland Way sign, to continue steeply up a narrow path to the top of the cliff. From here you follow a clear path across fields and over a succession of stiles, with fine views along the coast in both directions — Staithes is behind you and Runswick Bay lies ahead, backed by the headland of Kettleness. The path curves right and goes through a gate into Port Mulgrave, a nineteenth-century iron-ore port — a speculative Victorian venture that never really took off. Bear left along the road high above the small harbour, and, where the road bends right, bear left through a gate, at a Cleveland Way sign, to rejoin the coastal path.

Continue along the top of the cliffs, up and down steps at times and over several stiles, eventually turning right over a stile, at a Runswick Bay sign, and climbing another one a few yards on to head away from the coast. Keep along the edge of a field, by a hedge on the left, climb a stile and continue along the path ahead to come out by the side of the Runswick Bay Hotel at Runswick Bank Top. Walk downhill back into the village.

20 Osmotherley, Mount Grace Priory and Scarth Wood Moor

Start: Osmotherley

Distance: 7 miles (11.25 km). Omitting the detour to Mount Grace Priory, 5½ miles (8.75 km)

Approximate time: 3½ hours (2½ hours for the shorter version)

Parking: Village street in Osmotherley

Refreshments: Pubs and cafés at Osmotherley

Ordnance Survey maps: Landranger 93 (Middlesbrough & Darlington), 99 (Northallerton & Ripon) and 100 (Malton & Pickering), Outdoor Leisure 26 (North York Moors – Western area)

General description This is a walk with a decidedly ecclesiastical flavour, starting in a village that possesses both a medieval church and an eighteenth-century Methodist chapel, passing a restored Tudor chapel and providing an optional (but much recommended) detour to the superb and rare remains of a Carthusian monastery. It is also a grand scenic walk which proceeds along the edge of the Cleveland escarpment, continues over Scarth Wood Moor, with fine views of the Cleveland Hills, and returns along a section of the Hambleton Drove Road. There are several ascents but none that are either lengthy or strenuous.

The village of Osmotherley, a harmonious mixture of old and new, stands high up on the Cleveland escarpment overlooking the Vale of Mowbray. It has an attractive, if heavily restored, medieval church with an unusual Viking hogback tomb and one of the oldest Methodist chapels in the country, built in 1754 shortly after a visit by John Wesley. In the village centre is the Market Cross and a stone table; it was the latter that Wesley used for his preaching.

Start by the Market Cross and take the road signposted to Swainby, heading uphill out of the village. Look out for a Cleveland Way signpost on the left where you turn onto a broad track **(A)**, passing between modern houses. To the left there is a grand view of Osmotherley, backed by the distinctive, brooding shape of Black Hambleton. At a

viewpoint indicator, from where you look out across the Vale of Mowbray to the Pennines beyond, the track forks. The Cleveland Way continues ahead but you take the right-hand fork and, after ¼ mile (0.5 km), climb some steps and head across grass to the Lady Chapel, attached to a cottage. It was founded in the early sixteenth century and belonged to nearby Mount Grace Priory. After falling into ruin, it was rebuilt in 1960 by the Roman Catholic Church and is now used again for worship. Continue past the chapel along a path that skirts a wood on the right and turn left to a stile. Climb over and bear left, keeping by a wall on the left, and head downhill to rejoin the Cleveland Way by Chapel Wood Farm **(B)**.

At this point the main route continues by turning sharp right through a gate, but for the detour to Mount Grace Priory keep ahead through the farmyard, bear left through a gate at the end and continue along the path ahead. Pass through another gate, after which the path bends right and heads downhill by a hedge and wire fence on the left, and, as you descend, keep a wire fence on your left all the while to a conifer plantation. Continue along the right-hand edge of the plantation to a stile, climb over, bear right and descend through the trees to cross a footbridge at the bottom end. Climb a stile, head across a field, making for a gate in the far right-hand corner, go through it and turn right along the drive to the priory.

Mount Grace is a rare example of a Carthusian monastery. There were only nine in the whole of England and this is by far the most complete and best preserved of them. Unlike the other monastic orders, the Carthusians emphasised individual rather than communal prayers and activities, which distinctively affected the layout of their monasteries. The church is much smaller than normal and around it is a series of cells instead of the usual communal domestic buildings. Each monk spent most of the time in his own cell and meals were placed in a hatch, arranged at an angle so that the monk could not communicate with whoever brought the food. Mount Grace was founded at the end of the fourteenth century and dissolved by Henry VIII in 1539.

Retrace your steps uphill to Chapel Wood Farm **(B)**, turn left and go through a gate to continue along the main route. After passing through another gate, bear right off the main path, at a Cleveland Way sign, to enter the plantations of South Wood which, for a while, hide the extensive views across the vale to the left. Head uphill through the trees and then continue along the top edge of woodland, passing a disused quarry on the right. Soon you pass the strange-looking shapes of the British Telecom Microwave

Radio Station (which proudly proclaims that it stands at 982 feet (298 m) above sea level) and continue by a wall on the right. There are now fine views on both sides: to the left, over the wooded slopes of the escarpment, the flatter lands of Cleveland and Durham, and to the right the impressive contours of the Cleveland Hills, with Roseberry Topping standing out in the distance. The path bears right to go through two gates in quick succession, and soon after the second gate there is a fork. Here take the right-hand track which heads across Scarth Wood Moor, bearing right away from the trees. About 100 yards (92 m) after the track meets a wall on the left, turn right along another track which heads down to join a lane **(C)**.

Turn right along the lane for ½ mile (0.75 km); the expanse of water in front is Cod Beck Reservoir. Where the lane bends sharply right to a car park, continue over a footbridge and along the broad uphill track in front **(D)**, part of the Hambleton Drove Road. The track soon levels out and keeps by the left-hand edge of a plantation, Walk along it for 1¼ miles (2 km), passing through a gate and continuing straight ahead, with a fine view of Black Hambleton in front, turning right at a public footpath sign just before reaching a road **(E)**.

Walk along a path by a wire fence and line of trees on the right, go through a gate, keep ahead to pass through another gate and continue along the edge of a field by a wall on the left. Go through a gate at the end of that field, continue down a walled track and go through another gate, turning left along another track which descends to a Cleveland Way sign. Turn right over a stile here **(F)** and, after a few yards, continue along a broad track, bearing right to pass to the right of a farm. Climb a stile and continue downhill towards the thickly-wooded slopes ahead. Cross a track and continue over a footbridge into the trees, climbing the steep wooded ridge by a series of steps. At the top, keep ahead across a field, with Osmotherley church directly in front, go through two squeezer stiles and continue along a narrow path between hedges, passing through two more squeezer stiles. Cross a lane and continue along a path, passing in front of cottages and the Methodist chapel, under an archway and back into the village centre.

SCALE 1:25 000 or 2½ INCHES to 1 MILE

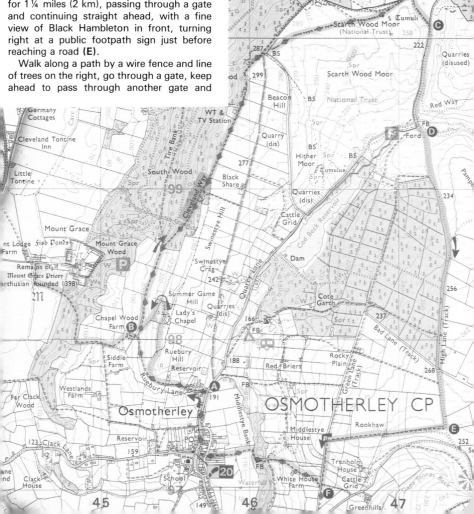

21 The Cook Monument and Roseberry Topping

Start:	Gribdale Gate car park
Distance:	6½ miles (10.5 km)
Approximate time:	3½ hours
Parking:	Gribdale Gate
Refreshments:	Pubs and cafés at Great Ayton
Ordnance Survey maps:	Landranger 93 (Middlesbrough & Darlington) and Outdoor Leisure 26 (North York Moors – Western area)

General description *To the east of Great Ayton lie two of the most prominent landmarks of the Cleveland Hills: the monument to Captain Cook on Easby Moor and the dramatic, 1,051 ft (320 m) Roseberry Topping, the most distinctive outline in the whole of the North York Moors and visible from many vantage points over a wide section of the moors and from the plain below. This walk incorporates both these features, as well as the village of Great Ayton. The climb to the Cook Monument is easy and gradual; in contrast the ascent of Roseberry Topping is much steeper and more strenuous.*

From the car park go through a gate at a Cleveland Way sign and head in a southerly direction along a broad track that follows the edge of Cleveland Forest. The track climbs steadily for ½ mile (0.75 km), eventually emerging into Easby Moor where you keep straight ahead to the Cook Monument **(A)**. This was erected in 1827 as a memorial to a man who lived in the area and who must have walked these moors as a boy before sailing off to much different climes. From this excellent vantage-point there are panoramic views over forest and moorland, hills and lowlands, the industries of Teesside and the ever-present Roseberry Topping.

At the monument turn right, not along the path at right-angles to your previous route but sharper right, along a narrower path that heads towards a wall by gateposts. Pass between the gateposts and continue, by a broken wall on the left, soon bearing left across rough grass down to the conifer plantation of Ayton Banks Wood. Continue steeply downhill through the trees and, as you descend, there are fine views of Great Ayton in front and the Cleveland Plain stretching away in the distance. At the bottom end of the plantation, go through a

gate and continue along the edge of a field by a wall on the right. Where that wall ends, turn right along a track that heads downhill, keeping by another wall on the right, to a gate. Go through and continue down a very pleasant, tree-lined path to a lane **(B)**.

Turn left along this lane for 1 mile (1.5 km), over a railway bridge and on to Great Ayton, following it as it curves right into the village to a T-junction. Here turn left if you wish to explore Great Ayton: a large, attractive and spacious village of fine old houses and wide greens, through which flows the River Leven. Captain Cook spent much of his early life here and the school which he attended is now a Cook Museum.

The route continues by turning right at the T-junction and, about 100 yards (92 m) further along the road, right again **(C)** through a kissing-gate at a public footpath sign. Keep ahead a short distance to go through another kissing-gate and walk across a field to a third one in a thicket straight ahead. Continue through the thicket, pass through another gate at the far end and keep along the edge of a field, by a hedge on the left, passing to the right of Cleveland Lodge. Continue in a straight line through three more kissing-gates and along the edge of the next field (by a hedge on the left), climbing two stiles and crossing the railway line. Keep ahead to climb another stile and continue along the edge of a field, by a wire fence on the left, following it round to the left and over a stile a few yards in front to enter Cliff Ridge Wood. Climb steeply through the wood to a metal gate at a junction of paths and turn half-right along a path that continues uphill, diagonally through the wood, to a stile. Climb over, turn right along the edge of a field to another stile, climb that and bear left downhill, by a wire fence on the right, to

climb another stile in that fence. Descend some steps and turn left along a tarmac farm road which heads uphill, passes to the right of Airy Holme Farm, curves left in front of the farm and then turns right, heading towards Roseberry Topping.

Pass through a gate, continue along a track and, where the track bears right, keep straight ahead along a grassy path to go through another gate. Turn left and now climb steeply to the summit **(D)**. Early prints show that Roseberry Topping had a perfect conical shape but subsidence, caused by the tunnelling of iron mines into the hill, led to the collapse of the western face — hence its present abrupt, but instantly recognisable, outline. As might be expected, the views from the summit are both impressive and extensive: a superb panorama that takes in the North Sea coast, Guisborough, Teesside, the Cleveland Plain, the Cleveland Hills, Great Ayton and the Cook Monument.

At the summit turn right along the ridge and follow a path steeply downhill, making for a wire fence and parallel broken wall.

Roseberry Topping's familiar and unmistakable outline

Keep by this wall, heading uphill again and passing the edge of a plantation, to a gate and footpath sign. Here continue, between the edge of Newton Moor and Great Ayton Moor on the left and the plantation on the right, along a path that keeps by the wall on the right all the way, gradually bearing right and descending to the road at Gribdale Gate.

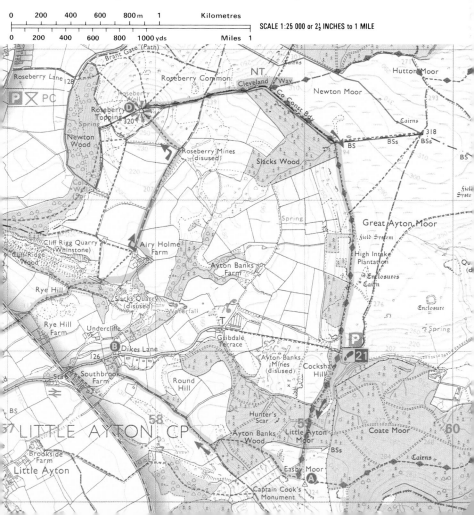

SCALE 1:25 000 or 2½ INCHES to 1 MILE

22 Broxa Forest, the River Derwent and Whisper Dales

Start:	Forestry Commission car park at Reasty Bank
Distance:	8 ½ miles (13.5 km)
Approximate time:	4 ½ hours
Parking:	Reasty Bank
Refreshments:	None
Ordnance Survey maps:	Landranger 94 (Whitby) and 101 (Scarborough & Bridlington), Outdoor Leisure 27 (North York Moors – Eastern area)

General description *This walk through Broxa Forest proves that conifer plantations, when sensibly planned and interspersed with older deciduous woodland, are not always gloomy and uninteresting but can provide attractive and varied walking. Starting at the fine viewpoint of Reasty Bank, the route proceeds along broad forest tracks to descend to the River Derwent. Then follows a most beautiful walk along the banks of the river, through a mixture of conifer woodland, meadowland and broad-leaved woodland, before heading across to the valley of Lowdales Beck and continuing through the lovely wooded Whisper Dales, finally climbing through the forest back to Reasty Bank.*

The starting point itself at Reasty Bank, on the edge of Broxa Forest, is a fine viewpoint, looking northwards over Harwood Dale and eastwards across to the coast just north of Scarborough. Begin by walking westwards along a broad forest track, initially parallel to the road on the right, following blue walker waymarks. Gaps in the trees on the right reveal a succession of superb views over Harwood Dale. Keep along the top of the ridge, bearing slightly right at a blue walker waymark (where the main track bears left), by the side of a forestry gate and along a narrow path. Continue in a straight line and, soon after bearing left, look out for a blue walker sign where you turn sharp right **(A)**, almost doubling back down a narrow path between dense conifers. Turn sharply left at a T-junction and sharp right at the next junction of paths, continuing downhill to another path junction near a footbridge **(B)**.

Here turn left to walk along the left bank of the River Derwent for the next 2¾ miles (4.5 km), a delightful route comprising three stages: first through mixed woodland, then

through a gate into a more open landscape of sloping meadows edged with trees and dotted with gorse, and finally through another gate to enter broad-leaved woodland. The path keeps fairly straight, mostly hugging the river-bank, though the Derwent itself meanders. Just before reaching a lane ahead, turn left uphill **(C)** along the edge of trees to climb Broxa Banks, from where there is a particularly striking view over the Derwent valley of rolling wooded hills, with the distinctive, conical-shaped Howden Hill standing out prominently. Near the top of the bank, continue along a clearly visible path through the trees, climbing steeply to a T-junction of paths where you continue uphill, through a gate and onto a lane.

Turn left and follow the lane through the hamlet of Broxa, turning right at a public footpath sign **(D)**, at the far end of the hamlet, along a track, continuing to a stile and another public footpath sign. Climb over, bear left and head diagonally across a field – there is no clear path – to climb a stile in the far corner. Continue along the edge of the next field by the top edge of woodland on the left, climb another stile and, just before the next stile (redundant because of a broken fence), turn left and look out for a partially-hidden stile in front. Climb it, bear right along a narrow but discernible woodland path and head steeply downhill, continuing along the edge of a field at the bottom of the woods and following the field edge round to the left (likely to be overgrown) and down to another stile. Climb over, turn left **(E)** along a farm road, cross a footbridge over a beck, climb

A forest track leads into quiet and gentle Whisper Dales

SCALE 1:25 000 or 2½ INCHES to 1 MILE

the stile immediately ahead, at a public footpath sign, and continue along a path towards Lowdales Farm.

Climb a stile just in front of the farmhouse, keep ahead past the farm, cross two footbridges and climb another stile. Then continue along the broad track which climbs gently through Whisper Dales, at first with the stream on the left and later on the right, over a succession of stiles – a lovely, green, tranquil, wooded valley with excellent views; a superb finale to the walk. After passing Whisper Dales Farm on the left, the track climbs more steeply to re-enter the forest and continues through the conifers back to the car park.

23 Robin Hood's Bay and Ravenscar

Start:	Robin Hood's Bay
Distance:	9 miles (14.5 km)
Approximate time:	4½ hours
Parking:	Robin Hood's Bay
Refreshments:	Pubs and cafés at Robin Hood's Bay, hotel at Ravenscar
Ordnance Survey maps:	Landranger 94 (Whitby) and Outdoor Leisure 27 (North York Moors – Eastern area)

General description *The track of the disused Whitby – Scarborough Railway makes it possible to devise a splendid circular coastal walk linking Robin Hood's Bay and Ravenscar. On the first part of the walk, the inland section, the track provides a quick and trouble-free route to Ravenscar, a superb vantage point from where the view over the bay is magnificent. The return route to Robin Hood's Bay keeps to the coastal path along a particularly spectacular section of the North Yorkshire coast. The first half is obviously flat and easy; the second half is rather more energetic.*

A jumble of red-roofed cottages clustered together below steep cliffs, with narrow winding lanes, passages and stepped paths leading down to the sea, make up the enchanting fishing village of Robin Hood's Bay. Its previous remoteness and inaccessibility not surprisingly made it a notorious haunt for smugglers and, like Staithes and other places along this coast, parts of the village have in the past been swept away by storms and had to be rebuilt. Its name comes from a tradition that at some time Robin Hood fled here to escape from his pursuers by boarding a fishing vessel but, as with all Robin Hood stories, there is no factual basis for it. An added attraction of Robin Hood's Bay is that, because of the narrow streets, no cars are allowed; motorists have to park at one of two main car parks at the top of the village.

The walk begins at the Station Car Park where you turn right past the former station buildings and follow a tarmac lane down to a road. Turn right for about 100 yards (92 m) and, where the road bends to the right, turn left through a gate **(A)** to join the track of the disused Whitby – Scarborough Railway, built in 1885, closed down in 1965 but happily converted into a footpath. Keep along the pleasantly tree-lined track for 4½ miles (7.25km) to Ravenscar, crossing several roads and passing under several bridges, sometimes through deep wooded cuttings and at other times along embankments, with fine views all the way over gentle wooded hills to the right and over the coast and prominent headland of Ravenscar to the left. Where the track swings back towards the coast, there is a particularly fine view over Robin Hood's Bay and, approaching Ravenscar, you can see the now-overgrown remains of disused alum quarries. After passing through some of these quarries, bear left to a T-junction of paths and turn right along a paved path up to the road **(B)**, passing a National Trust Information Centre on the left. In the late nineteenth century there were grandiose plans to develop Ravenscar as a major resort, but they came to nothing, one of the reasons being the instability of the rocks in the area. The most notable building is the Raven Hall Hotel on the headland, built in the eighteenth century (and once visited by George III) and enlarged in the nineteenth century. It occupies the site of a Roman signal station.

On reaching the road, immediately turn left down a broad track, signposted 'Public Footpath to the Shore', to the left of the entrance to the Raven Hall Hotel. From this track there is the finest view of the walk, across the broad sweep of Robin Hood's Bay to the buildings of the village huddled together on the far side. Pass below the hotel walls to the right and follow the path as it curves sharply to the left **(C)** at a finger-post, following directions to Robin Hood's Bay.

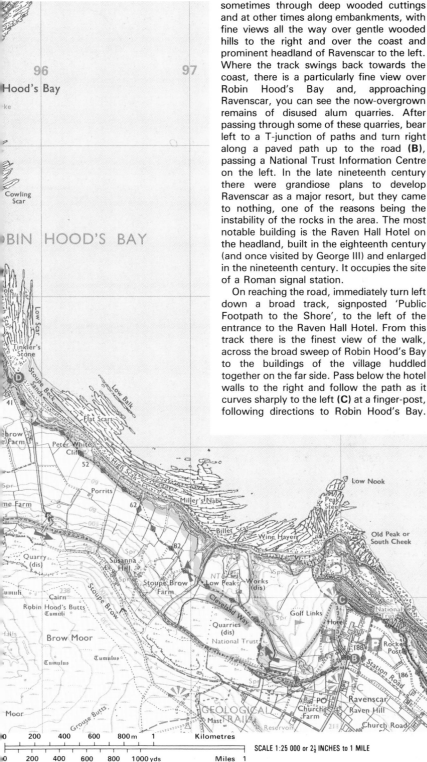

This part of the walk can be quite hazardous at times as it crosses the Raven Hall golf course. Shortly afterwards the path bends to the right to run parallel to the coast and, soon after descending into a wooded area, joins the Cleveland Way coming in from the left.

Keep along the Cleveland Way for 3½ miles (5.5 km) back to Robin Hood's Bay — a well-waymarked, easy to follow route, with plenty of Cleveland Way signs, which passes over several stiles and has that magnificent view over the bay ahead all the while. Nearing Robin Hood's Bay, the path meets a lane; turn right **(D)** along it for a few yards and then continue downhill along a paved path through a wooded dell, over a footbridge at the bottom by a small shingle beach, and steeply up steps on the other side onto the cliff top. Now the path hugs the edge of the cliffs, before descending steeply into Boggle Hole **(E)**. Cross the beck here by a footbridge, continue up the steep flight of steps in front, the stiffest climb of the walk, and keep ahead to soon regain the cliff edge. Climb a stile and, with a lovely view of the picturesque village huddled below, drop down through trees into Robin Hood's Bay and walk through its amazing jumble of narrow streets and alleys steeply uphill back to the Station Car Park.

Descending into Robin Hood's Bay from the coast path

24 Sutton Bank, White Horse of Kilburn and Gormire Lake

Start:	National Park Information Centre at Sutton Bank
Distance:	8 miles (12.75 km)
Approximate time:	4 hours
Parking:	Sutton Bank
Refreshments:	Café at Sutton Bank (restricted winter opening)
Ordnance Survey maps:	Landranger 100 (Malton & Pickering) and Outdoor Leisure 26 (North York Moors — Western area)

General description *A large proportion of the route can be seen from the starting point at Sutton Bank: to the left the almost vertical cliff of Roulston Scar, hiding the White Horse of Kilburn; below, the still, tree-fringed waters of Gormire Lake; and to the right the Cleveland Way heading northwards along the edge of the escarpment above Sutton Brow and Whitestone Cliff. As much of the walk is along the escarpment of the Hambleton Hills, it is inevitable that the views throughout are extensive and outstanding. Equally inevitable is that, having descended from the escarpment by the side of the White Horse, there is a long and steep ascent to regain it.*

The walk starts at the National Park Information Centre at the top of Sutton Bank, one of the most notorious ascents in the country for motorists (1 in 4 with hairpin bends), but also one of the most superb viewpoints, looking down the steep wooded slopes to Gormire Lake and then across the flat and fertile lands of the Vale of York towards the line of the Pennines on the distant horizon. It is also a popular place for both gliders and hang-gliders.

Cross the main road and take the path almost opposite the turning to Cold Kirby and Old Byland, signposted 'White Horse Walk'. The path follows the edge of the escarpment for 1½ miles (2.5 km), at first by the edge of a plantation on the left and later skirting a small airfield belonging to the Yorkshire Gliding Club. It continues above Roulston Scar and across the top of the White Horse, with superb views to the south over the Vale of Pickering to the Wolds beyond, turning right almost immediately afterwards and descending by steps to a lane and car park **(A)**. From here there is a good view of the White Horse, the brainchild of a local

Quarry (dis)
Quarries (dis)
Hall
143
Iggon Howl
113
Southwoods Hall
Midge Holm Gate
129
Southwoods Farm
114
South Woods
Pheasant Covert
Skipton Hill
169
142
Quarry (dis)
84
Southwoods Lodge
Skipton Hill
144
154
Whitestone Cliff or White Mare Crag
Cleaves House
Fairies Parlour (Cave)
Garbutt Wood
NATURE TRAIL
Gormire Rigg
GORMIRE LAKE
Great Relief Pot
Surton Brow
Cliff Plantation
Cairn
Gormire Farm
156
Quarry (dis)
CP
High Cleaves Farm
High Rigg
202
83
Surton Bank
High Rigg
169
132
Valley View
A 170
124
Quarry (dis)
Cragg House
235
Kennycow
128
MS
Hood Grange
Happy Valley
Hood Beck
Cragg Hall
HOOD GRANGE CP
Waterfall
82
Knowlson's Drop
99
Cave
Gliding Club
Hood Hill Plantation
Earthwork
Roulston Scar
Fort
Ivy Scar
Low Town Brow
Hood Hill
Hag Wood
WHITE HORSE WALK
Quarry (dis)
Silver Fox Farm
Hoodhill Field Plantation
Quarry (dis)
Quarry (dis)
High Ground Barn
Penfoot Wood
Acre House
117
50
Spruce Bank Wood
51
Little Acre
Oldstead Road
52
125
Scawling
en Stocking

HAMBLETON HILLS
Back Lane
Quarry (dis)
Chapel Cotta
304
303
304
Hambleton Down
Dialstone Plantation
299
Mast
Limekiln Plantation
274
265
Dialstone Farm
Quarry (dis)
High Quarry Plantation
294
Tumulus
Hambleton High House
Resr
324
Quarry (dis)
297
Hambleton House
283
Cold Kirby Moor
310
Garbutt Farm
Flassen Gill Slack
Hotel Plantation
Cote Moor
Hambleton Plantation
24
263
i P PC
PH
274
282
T
Kilburn Moor Plantation
Hambleton
Quarries (dis)
Spring Cottage
Tumuli
Spring Cot Farm
Easten Gill
Quarries (dis)
298
Shaw's Gate
Shaw's
Cleveland Way
Tumulus
High Town Bank Road
Low Town Bank Road
Raver
High Town Brow
Hell Hole
Scotch Corne
FBs
Coal Pit (dis)
Brookfield Farm
Quarry (dis)
132
Resr
180

0   200   400   600   800 m   1   Kilometres
0   200   400   600   800   1000 yds   Miles   1

SCALE 1:25 000 or 2½ INCHES to 1 MILE

Victorian schoolmaster, John Hodgson, and his friend, Thomas Taylor, who wanted to recreate here the white horses which had impressed them on the chalk downlands of southern England. Hodgson organised his pupils to mark it out in the limestone in 1857; it is 314 feet (95 m) long and 228 feet (69 m) high.

Continue ahead along the lane which winds downhill between trees for just over ½ mile (0.75 km) and, at the bottom of the hill, turn right along a broad track at a public bridle-way sign **(B)**. Where the track turns left to a farm, continue along the grassy path which climbs through plantations to join a well-surfaced forestry track. To the right is an impressive view of the sheer cliffs of Roulston Scar towering above the trees, an indication of how far you have descended. Continue to a fork, keep ahead and, soon after where you first see a farm across the fields in front, bear right off the track, at a bridle-way sign, along a narrow path, between trees on the left and a wire fence on the right, to a gate. Go through, turn left and head straight across the fields below Sutton Bank towards the farm, turning left at a bridle-way sign just before it and keeping by a wire fence on the right. Pass to the left of the farmhouse and, at the next bridle-way sign, turn right through a gate, cross a footbridge and keep straight ahead to another gate. Go through that, climb a stile almost opposite and continue, by a wire fence on the left, over another stile and onto the main road **(C)**.

Turn right along the road for just over ¼ mile (0.5 km) — there are wide verges on both sides — ignoring a public footpath sign on the left and turning left at a public bridle-way sign **(D)** along a broad track which heads up, passing Gormire Farm on the left, to Gormire Lake. Despite its proximity to a main road and well-frequented walking area, the lake has a decidedly remote and mysterious atmosphere. It was formed as a result of a glacial landslip and is unusual in that it does not have an inlet or outlet, appearing to be entirely regulated by underground drainage. Go through a gate and bear right along a grassy wooded path that keeps above the right-hand edge of the lake. After briefly joining the lakeshore, the path bears right through trees to reach Southwoods Lodge.

Here bear right through a gate and along the broad track ahead — at a public bridle-way sign — which keeps below the line of the escarpment on the right. Soon Southwoods Hall is seen ahead and, at a junction of tracks called Midge Holm Gate **(E)**, keep ahead along a track that bears right in front of the hall. Where that track curves left to the hall, keep straight ahead, go through a gate into a farmyard and turn sharply right between barns down to another gate. Pass through that and continue, by a wall on the left, to a marker-post. Following blue arrows, turn right and left and right again, heading uphill to another marker-post. Now comes the most challenging part of the walk. Keep ahead to go through a gate and continue, now climbing quite steeply, to another gate with a blue arrow, on the edge of a plantation. Go through and continue through the plantation, climbing steeply to reach a broad forest track. Bear right along it for a few yards and then turn sharp left to continue the upward journey through the dense plantations, to arrive at a gate at the top edge of the trees.

Go through and turn left along the track, which bears gradually right uphill to the top of the scarp to meet a broad grassy track **(F)**. This is part of the Cleveland Way and you turn right along it to end the walk as you started it, with an exhilarating ramble of nearly 2 miles (3.25 km) along the top of the scarp back to Sutton Bank, with magnificent views to the right all the way.

The extensive view across the Vale of York from the White Horse of Kilburn

25 Goathland, Mallyan Spout and the Roman road

The Roman road across Wheeldale Moor

Start:	Goathland
Distance:	8 miles (12.75 km). Shorter versions 6½ miles (10.5 km) and 2½ miles (4 km)
Approximate time:	4½ hours (3½ and 1½ hours for the shorter versions)
Parking:	Goathland
Refreshments:	Pubs and cafés at Goathland, pub-cum-café at Beck Hole
Ordnance Survey maps:	Landranger 94 (Whitby) and Outdoor Leisure 27 (North York Moors — Eastern area)

General description *Both a wide range of scenery and considerable historic appeal are featured in this superb and fairly long, but not particularly strenuous, walk. The climbing that is involved is not steep or lengthy and, if neither time nor energy allow for the full walk, two shorter versions are provided, the 6½-mile (10.5 km) version starting at the southern end of the village, beside the Mallyan Spout Hotel. The scenic variety includes a narrow wooded gorge, spectacular waterfall and stretches of bare and open moorland, with inevitably extensive vistas. The historic interest comes from the fact that the route utilises two former transport systems, very different in nature and about 1900 years apart in time – an exceptionally well-preserved stretch of Roman road and the track of a nineteenth-century railway.*

Refer to map overleaf.

In Goathland the moors are inseparable from the village. Sheep graze on the spacious commons, keeping them close-cropped and tidy, and the widely-spaced cottages are strung out along a ¾ mile (1.25 km) ridge above the valleys of Ellerbeck to the east and West Beck to the west. The squat, solid-looking church at the southern end of the village, built in 1896, harmonises perfectly with its surroundings.

The walk starts at the car park where you turn left along the road and, after about 200 yards (184 m), left again through a gate at a signpost marked 'Grosmont Rail Trail'. For the next mile (1.5 km) you follow the track of the original Whitby – Pickering Railway, built by George Stephenson and opened in 1836, to Beck Hole, gently descending the 1 in 15 incline. What is initially a grassy track becomes a stony tree-lined track after

crossing a road, making a most attractive walk. The incline between Beck Hole and Goathland was a major problem for the railway — it was too steep for both the early horses and later steam locomotives; the problem could only be solved by hauling the carriages up it by means of a cable system. This proved both unsatisfactory and unsafe and therefore in 1865 an alternative route, the one used by the present North Yorkshire Moors Railway, was created by blasting a cutting through the rocks to the north.

Approaching Beck Hole, go through a gate and keep ahead for a few yards before turning left through another gate in front of Incline Cottage (**A**). (The hamlet is about ¼ mile (0.5 km) further on, reached by turning right through a gate.) Follow a path across a field, by the beck on the right, to a stile. Climb over and for the next ½ mile (0.75 km) keep along the right-hand edge of fields, climbing steps to the top edge of the woods that clothe the steep sides of the beck on the right and continuing over a series of stiles, before descending to a footbridge and entering the woods. Shortly afterwards you pass a path on the left.

Those wanting to do the short version should turn along this path that leads back to Goathland. Alternatively those who wish to do a longer but not the full walk can join the walk here by starting off along this path from the southern end of Goathland village by the side of the Mallyan Spout Hotel.

Keep ahead for the next mile (1.5 km) along a sometimes rocky and quite slippery and dangerous path by the side of West Beck, through an outstandingly beautiful, steep-sided, wooded valley, soon passing the impressive 70 feet (21 m) fall of Mallyan Spout. Continue past the fall, ascending and descending and keeping by the rocky waters of the beck all the while, to eventually climb a stile onto a lane by a bridge (**B**).

Turn left along the lane and, where it bends to the left, turn right through a metal gate, at a public bridle-way sign, along a

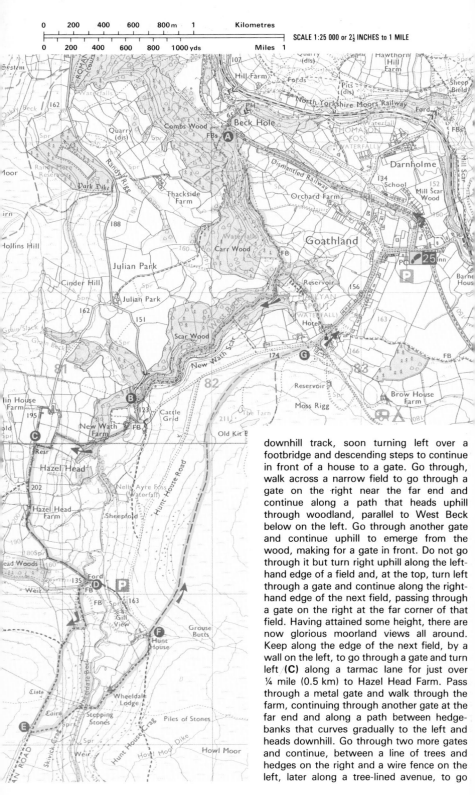

downhill track, soon turning left over a footbridge and descending steps to continue in front of a house to a gate. Go through, walk across a narrow field to go through a gate on the right near the far end and continue along a path that heads uphill through woodland, parallel to West Beck below on the left. Go through another gate and continue uphill to emerge from the wood, making for a gate in front. Do not go through it but turn right uphill along the left-hand edge of a field and, at the top, turn left through a gate and continue along the right-hand edge of the next field, passing through a gate on the right at the far corner of that field. Having attained some height, there are now glorious moorland views all around. Keep along the edge of the next field, by a wall on the left, to go through a gate and turn left **(C)** along a tarmac lane for just over ¼ mile (0.5 km) to Hazel Head Farm. Pass through a metal gate and walk through the farm, continuing through another gate at the far end and along a path between hedge-banks that curves gradually to the left and heads downhill. Go through two more gates and continue, between a line of trees and hedges on the right and a wire fence on the left, later along a tree-lined avenue, to go through another gate. Now walk along a narrow grassy path which heads down to the beck **(D)**.

Keep ahead for a few yards and turn left over a footbridge, then turn right alongside the beck to climb a stile and continue to a 'Roman Road' footpath sign. Here turn left, in the direction of the sign, heading up over rough grassland and bearing right to climb a stile. Continue along the edge of the next field (by a wall on the left), curving slightly left to go through a metal gate, and ahead is the Roman road (or Wade's Causeway) which you walk beside for the next ½ mile (0.75 km) across the open and breezy moorland of Wheeldale Moor, with extensive views all around. This is one of the best-preserved and most impressive stretches of Roman road in Britain, its culverts and parallel ditches still visible. It was built around AD 80 and was part of a route across the moors from the fort at Malton to the North Sea coast, though its exact northern termination is uncertain – possibly it was at one of the chain of coastal signal stations.

After climbing a stile, continue along the Roman road for about another 300 yards (276 m) and, opposite a sign warning you not to deface the monument, turn sharp left **(E)** along a clear path through the heather, which soon descends by a group of rocks (Skivick Crag) to some stepping-stones over Wheeldale Beck. Cross them, continue over a stile and turn left, following a path past the right-hand edge of a large house, Wheeldale Lodge – now a youth hostel. Continue by a wall on the left, bearing slightly left to drop down over a beck to a tarmac lane by Hunt House. Keep along this lane for a few yards, then bear half-right **(F)** and head across open moorland, gradually bearing right and making for the line of crags ahead.

At this point there is no one obvious path but a number of indistinct paths and sheep tracks – just make for the craggy ridge ahead and then bear left to follow the top edge of the ridge, with magnificent views over the valley to the left and bare heathery moorland to the right. The path is now easy to follow, keeping along the edge of the ridge roughly parallel to the road below on the left. Make for a prominent cairn in front and here bear first left (several paths again) and then right into a shallow valley along a path that runs parallel to the road. The path curves gently to the right, drawing closer to the road all the while, and soon the houses of Goathland can be seen ahead. By now the path has become grassy, clear and easy to follow once more. Finally descend to the road near Goathland church **(G)** and continue for nearly ¾ mile (1.25 km) through the long and widely-scattered village back to the starting point.

26 Westerdale Moor

Start:	Westerdale
Distance:	11 miles (17.5 km)
Approximate time:	6 hours
Parking:	Roadside parking in Westerdale
Refreshments:	Lion Inn at Blakey
Ordnance Survey maps:	Landranger 94 (Whitby) and Outdoor Leisure 26 (North York Moors – Western area)

General description *Westerdale, the name of the upper reaches of Eskdale and one of the remoter parts of the North York Moors, is surrounded by lofty moorland and has a lonely grandeur that is strikingly appealing. The first part of the walk mainly keeps by the infant River Esk below the wild and empty slopes of Westerdale Moor, heading up to join the track of the disused Rosedale Ironstone Railway which is followed to Blakey Ridge and from which there are the most superb views down Farndale. The route then continues around the head of Rosedale, passing two of the numerous crosses that were used as waymarks by earlier travellers on the moors, before returning to Westerdale. This is a magnificent moorland walk but some rough terrain is encountered and, unless experienced in the use of a compass, it is advisable not to attempt it in poor, especially misty, weather.*

Refer to map on page 71.

Although little more than a cluster of houses around a nineteenth-century church, Westerdale appears almost as an urban oasis amidst the remote and empty moors and makes an excellent centre for some particularly challenging rambles. In the village centre turn down a lane signposted 'Youth Hostel', passing the church on the left, and immediately in front is a splendid moorland view – an almost permanent feature of this walk. Follow the curving lane to the right and left, passing the youth hostel, formerly a Victorian country lodge, on the right and continue past Hall Farm along what has now become a narrow tarmac track. Drop down over the River Esk and keep along the track, turning right and passing through two gates.

After the second gate, turn left along a farm track **(A)** and, where the track bends right and starts to ascend to New House Farm, turn left through a gate, at a public footpath sign, and follow a clear path across two fields. Cross a footbridge over a beck and continue across the next field, with the river on the left, climbing two stiles and continuing across a field to a farm road. Cross the road, keep ahead a few yards to climb another stile and head across a field towards Wood End Farm in front. Go through a gate on the right to pass behind the farmhouse, pass through another gate and continue, by farm buildings on the left, to a stile. Climb over, cross a footbridge and continue by the river to another footbridge by a ford (B). Turn left over it and immediately turn right at a footpath sign to Farndale.

For the next 1½ miles (2.5 km) the path keeps close to the River Esk on the right in a more or less straight line, passing through gates and over stiles, through a strikingly beautiful and increasingly wild and open landscape below the slopes of Westerdale Moor. Eventually it crosses a footbridge over the river and continues along the other bank, heading up to a stile. Climb over and continue, slightly uphill and away from the river, to pass between gate posts. Keep along the edge of the next field, veering away from a wall on the right to go through a gap in the wall ahead. Pass by the ruins of a former farm (Esklets), continue along a track, cross a stream and keep ahead a few yards to where the track turns sharp right (C). Follow it uphill, soon bearing left and continuing across open moorland up to a footpath sign (D).

Here turn left to join the track of the former Rosedale Ironstone Railway, built in the nineteenth century to carry iron ore from the mines around Rosedale to the River Tees.

Fat Betty (alternatively called White Cross) still guides walkers across the heathery expanses between Rosedale and Westerdale

Nowadays it is a superb, high-level moorland route which gives the most magnificent views as it loops around the head of Farndale. This section of it is one of the easier parts of the Lyke Wake Walk, a strenuous 40 mile (64 km) east – west challenge across the moors which has to be accomplished in one day. After nearly 2 miles (3.25 km), turn left off the track at a Lyke Wake Walk sign and follow an uphill path through the heather. Soon you join a wall on the right and you keep by it as it curves to the right, passing the burial mound of Blakey Howe, to reach the road by the Lion Inn (E).

Turn left along the road for 1 mile (1.5 km) – the road runs along Blakey Ridge which separates Farndale from Rosedale – as far as the Margery Bradley Stone on the left (F), an old marker-stone for travellers across the moors. Here turn right, at a public bridle-way sign, along a path that winds through heather across the head of Rosedale, with superb views to the right down the dale. The path curves gradually to the left to meet another road (G) near another marker-stone, called White Cross (or alternatively Fat Betty). Cross over and, at a public bridle-way sign, continue along a path that passes to the right of Fat Betty across more expanses of moorland for ½ mile (0.75 km), keeping in a straight line and following a series of boundary stones, down to a road (H).

Keep ahead along this road for ¾ mile (1.25 km), from which there are splendid views all around – Danby Dale on the right, Eskdale ahead, Commondale Moor to the left, and even Roseberry Topping can be seen peeping above the horizon. Where a side-road branches off to the right, turn left at a public bridle-way sign (J), passing to the right of High Stone Dyke, an earthwork topped by a boundary stone. Follow a narrow path through heather, descending to a gate in front of a farm. Go through, keep ahead for a few yards and, at a tree, turn left between the farm buildings, turning sharp right through a gate to pass in front of the farmhouse (the route is clearly waymarked). At a bridle-way sign, bear right through the right-hand one of a pair of gates and walk along the edge of a field, by a wall on the left, heading downhill to a small wood. Bear right to continue down through the trees, cross a stream and go through a metal gate and across a field to pass through another metal gate. Keep ahead along the edge of the next field, by a wall on the left, go through another gate and continue, this time by a wall on the right, towards Broad Gate Farm. Continue through two more gates, past the farm buildings and along a tarmac farm road for ½ mile (0.75 km), turning left (K) at a crossroads along a lane into Westerdale village to conclude a memorable walk.

1:32 000 or 2 INCHES to 1 MILE

| 0 | 200 | 400 | 600 | 800 m² | 1 | | Kilometres |

| 0 | 200 | 400 | 600 | 800 | 1000 yds | | Miles |

27 Cold Moor and Urra Moor

Start:	Chop Gate
Distance:	9 miles (14.5 km)
Approximate time:	5 hours
Parking:	Chop Gate (just to the south of the hamlet)
Refreshments:	Pub at Chop Gate
Ordnance Survey maps:	Landranger 93 (Middlesbrough & Darlington) and 100 (Malton & Pickering), Outdoor Leisure 26 (North York Moors – Western area)

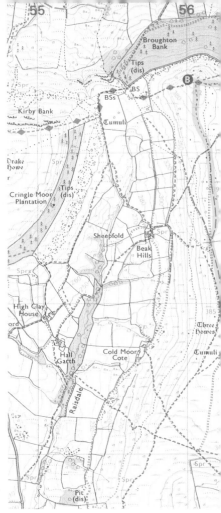

General description *This is a walk, mostly across the exposed moorlands of the Cleveland Hills near the head of Bilsdale, that should only be attempted in good weather. It is also quite a strenuous walk, involving a lot of 'up and down' work, but as compensation there are glorious and expansive views all the way. From Chop Gate you proceed over the at times aptly-named Cold Moor to the northern edge of the Cleveland escarpment. Here you turn east to follow a section of the Cleveland Way along the escarpment, then southwards along the edge of barren Urra Moor and finally descend back into Bilsdale. Not only are the views expansive, they are also varied: glimpses of urban and industrialised Teesside in the distance contrasting with both the sparsely-populated gentleness of Bilsdale and the severity and bleakness of the surrounding high moorland.*

Walk along the main road into the hamlet of Chop Gate, pronounced locally 'Chop Yat', once an important meeting-place of moorland tracks and now an excellent walking centre. Turn left along the lane signposted to Carlton and immediately turn right **(A)**, at a public bridle-way sign, along a track which passes the Wesleyan Chapel on the right and continues between banks – later becoming a wide green lane which leads up to a gate. Go through and keep ahead, gently ascending and passing through another gate onto the open moor. Continue parallel to the wall on the right for about 100 yards (92 m) and, after the wall bears right, keep along a narrow but distinct path through bracken, heather and rough grass, climbing all the while.

At first the path keeps roughly parallel with a plantation on the right, then it continues straight ahead, later becoming wider and ascending Cold Moor. As you are now walking along a wide ridge, the views on both sides over the rolling moorlands are

superb. Keep ahead to the highest point, marked by a small cairn, where you reach the northern edge of the Cleveland escarpment and a T-junction of paths **(B)**. Ahead is a magnificent view over the Cleveland Plain with Stokesley below, the industries of Teesside in the distance and the distinctive shape of Roseberry Topping dominating the scene.

Now follows the main 'up and down' part of the walk. Turn right to join the Cleveland Way, descending steeply to a gate. Go through and keep ahead, climbing even more steeply up Hasty Bank to a prominent group of rocks, the Wain Stones – from where there are even more magnificent views. Continue along the top of the scarp before dropping down steeply again to a stile, climb over and turn right by a wall on the right, later descending some steps to the Helmsley – Stokesley road **(C)**.

Cross over, pass through a gate on the other side, by a Cleveland Way sign, and continue along an uphill path, by a wall on

Bilsdale — green and fertile but encircled by forbidding moors

the left that borders a plantation. Go through a gate and keep ahead, still climbing by the wall on the left, continuing more steeply through a narrow rocky cleft to go through a gate in a wall. Keep ahead for about 50 yards (46 m) and then turn right **(D)** along a faint, grassy narrow path, just above the wall on the right that you have passed through. Ahead are the bleak expanses of Urra Moor. The path, now clearer, bears left across the heathery moorland and then curves right, following for the next 2 miles (3.25 km) a man-made earthwork of uncertain (possibly Iron Age) origin on the right — though at times the earthwork is not very clear and occasionally disappears altogether. Continue along the edge of the moor, turning right to descend into a gully, crossing a stream and turning right again on the other side. At this point a large proportion of the route can be surveyed: ahead is the long ridge of Cold Moor on the western side of Bilsdale, to the right of that is Hasty Bank, and the gap to the right of Hasty Bank reveals more distant

views of Teesside and, later on, Roseberry Topping.

The path keeps straight ahead, joining a wall on the right for a while and, past the end of that wall, continues to a junction of paths by a notice-board on the left asking you not to damage the moorland. Continue, still with the earthwork on the right, passing a plantation on the right and ascending to a rocky ridge. At the top you meet a broad track: bear right along it, follow it down to a wall, turn left and, after about 50 yards (46 m), turn right along a track to a footpath sign to William Beck. Here turn right **(E)** down to a gate, go through and continue, descending between heather and bracken, through another gate, across a field, through another gate and down a walled track to pass through one more gate and on to William Beck Farm. By the side of the farmhouse, turn left along a straight track and follow it for ½ mile (0.75 km) to a gate and onto the main road. Turn right for the short distance back to Chop Gate.

28 Ingleby Moor and Greenhow Bank

Start:	Ingleby Greenhow
Distance:	10½ miles (16.75 km)
Approximate time:	5½ hours
Parking:	By church in Ingleby Greenhow
Refreshments:	Pub at Ingleby Greenhow
Ordnance Survey maps:	Landranger 93 (Middlesbrough & Darlington) and 94 (Whitby), Outdoor Leisure 26 (North York Moors — Western area)

General description *There is a tremendously exhilarating feeling on this fine and lengthy walk across open, sweeping and remote moorland. The walk recalls the heyday of the nineteenth-century iron-mining boom and makes use of both an old coach road and a disused railway line. Despite its length and the wildness of much of the terrain, there are just two climbs to be negotiated, and only one of these, up Ingleby Bank, is steep. The descent of Greenhow Bank is via the Ingleby Incline, down which wagons laden with iron ore used to be lowered, until the line closed in 1928. The views are superb throughout but, unless you are an experienced walker able to use a compass, this is definitely a walk to be set aside for a fine, settled day.*

Refer to map overleaf.

Nowadays it is almost impossible to envisage the small, quiet and remote village of Ingleby Greenhow, nestling in a fold of the Cleveland Hills at the foot of a steep, wooded embankment, as a busy and noisy industrial centre; but from 1861 to 1928 it occupied a key position in the transportation of iron ore from the mines around Rosedale to the furnaces of Teesside and Durham. A major problem was how to get the ore from the high moorland down the steep escarpment to the Tees and this was solved in 1861 by building a railway across the moors from Rosedale to the top of Greenhow Bank, down which the wagons were lowered by means of a rope-worked incline in order that they could continue on to Middlesbrough. Since the line closed in 1928 the village has largely reverted to its previous sleepy existence.

The walk starts by the church, a small plain building with a low squat tower, which dates from the twelfth century and, though largely rebuilt in the eighteenth century, retains its fine and rare Norman nave. From the church

walk to a T-junction and turn right along the road signposted to Kildale and Castleton. After about 100 yards (92 m), turn right **(A)**, at a public footpath sign, along a narrow path, by a house on the left, to a stile. Climb over and bear left along the edge of a field, climbing another stile and continuing by the boundary fences of gardens on the left. Pass through a gap into the next field and head straight across it down to a stile and footpath sign. Climb over and walk along the edge of the next field, by a hedge, wire fence and stream on the right; over to the right is a view of Ingleby Manor. At a footpath sign, climb the stile in front, turn left to immediately climb another stile and continue along the edge of a field (by a wire fence on the left), over another stile and on to a gate at the end of the next field. Go through, turn right along a farm road, keeping to the right of Bank Foot Farm, where the tarmac road becomes a rough track, and continue up to a gate.

Now comes the steep climb up Ingleby Bank. Go through the gate and follow the track uphill through a plantation, passing through a gate at the top end of the trees and continuing upwards, a climb of nearly ½ mile (0.75 km). At the top of the bank by Battersby Crag, there is an extensive and varied view over farmland, hill and moor, with both the Cook Monument and Roseberry Topping standing out prominently. At this point the broad stony track turns sharp right but you continue straight ahead along a grassy path which climbs more gently now, winding between heather and grass to the top of the ridge where you meet a broad, straight, sandy track by a small cairn **(B)**.

This is the Cleveland Way; cross over it and continue along the path opposite which bears slightly right and heads across the wide, open, heathery expanses of Ingleby Moor, descending into a shallow valley to cross a beck, climbing gently on the other side for a while, then flattening out and continuing across the wild and lonely moorland, with magnificent views all around. Look out for where the path bends right and follow it down to join a broad track on the rim of the valley ahead. Bear right along this track for a few yards to a small cairn **(C)**. (If you meet this track at a different point, just bear right along it until you reach the cairn.)

At the cairn, bear right again along a path (Middle Head Top) that heads uphill, at first curving gently to the left and, after passing some rocks, continuing more or less in a straight line towards the Bronze Age burial chamber of Burton Howe on the rise ahead. Drop down a few yards to rejoin the Cleveland Way and turn left along a broad track **(D)**, once an old coach road across the moors between Stokesley and Kirbymoorside. Follow it for about 1¼ miles (2 km)

across the top of Greenhow Bank, passing the Jenny Bradley Stone, an old marker-stone to guide travellers across the moors, to reach a junction of tracks called Bloworth Crossing (E). This remote spot was where the coach road crossed the Rosedale Ironstone Railway and from here the panoramic views over wild and empty moorland are magnificent.

Here you turn sharp right to join the track of the old ironstone railway and keep along it for just over ¾ mile (1.25 km) to the top of the Ingleby Incline, where there are the foundations of a winding-house. Walk down the incline — from which there are superb views ahead across the plain to the industries of Teesside — climb a stile and keep ahead, between the conifers of Battersby Plantation, down to the bottom of Greenhow Bank. Continue along the pleasant tree-lined track for another ¾ mile (1.25 km), going through a gate and passing some old railwaymen's cottages on the right.

Just after passing a wood on the left, look out for a stile (F), climb it and head straight across the field in front to a stile by a gate. Climb that, continue along the edge of the next field, by a hedge and wire fence on the left, to climb another stile and continue over a footbridge. Bear right along a track up to Woods Farm, go through two metal gates to pass in front of the farmhouse on the right and continue along the track to a lane. Turn right, turn right again at a public footpath sign (G) along a drive towards a farm and, just in front of the farm buildings, turn left at another footpath sign. Climb a stile in front and then follow yellow waymarks around the edge of a field to climb another stile.

Head across the middle of the next field,

climbing a stile at the far end by a group of trees and near a farmhouse. Pass in front of the farmhouse, climb another stile and continue towards a belt of trees on the right. Climb a stile, bear left along the edge of the wood, climb one more stile and continue along a narrow path, between a wire fence on the left and the wood on the right, to a gate. Go through, descend some steps to a track and turn right over the footbridge, by a ford, to Ingleby Greenhow church a few yards ahead.

The Cleveland escarpment at Ingleby Bank

Useful organisations

The Countryside Commission,
John Dower House, Crescent Place,
Cheltenham, Gloucestershire GL50 3RA.
Tel: 0242 21381

The National Trust
36 Queen Anne's Gate, London SW1H
9AS. Tel: 071-222 9251
(Yorkshire Regional Office, 27 Tadcaster
Road, York YO2 2QG. Tel: 0904 702021)

Council for National Parks,
45 Shelton Street, London WC2H 9HS.
Tel: 071-240 3603

North York Moors National Park,
The Old Vicarage, Bondgate, Helmsley,
York YO6 5BP. Tel: 0439 70657

National Park Authority Visitor Centres
can be found at:

Danby Lodge (Tel: 0287 60654)

Sutton Bank (Tel: 0845 597426)

Pickering (Tel: 0751 73791)

Ryedale Folk Museum at Hutton-le-Hole
(Tel: 07515 367)

Ravenscar (Tel: 0723 870138)

Yorkshire and Humberside Tourist Board,
312 Tadcaster Road, York YO2 2HF.
Tel: 0904 707961

North York Moors Association,
7 The Avenue, Nunthorpe,
Middlesbrough, Cleveland TS7 0AA.
Tel: 0642 316412

The Ramblers' Association,
1/5 Wandsworth Road, London SW8
2LJ. Tel: 071-582 6878

The Forestry Commission,
Information Branch, 231 Corstorphine
Road, Edinburgh EH12 7AT.
Tel: 031 334 0303

The Youth Hostels Association,
Trevelyan House, 8 St Stephen's Hill,
St Albans, Hertfordshire AL1 2DY.
Tel: 0727 55215

The Long Distance Walkers' Association,
Lodgefield Cottage, High Street,
Flimwell, Wadhurst, East Sussex TN5
7PH. Tel: 058 087 341

The Council for the Protection of Rural
England,
4 Hobart Place, London SW1W 0HY.
Tel: 071-235 5959

Ordnance Survey,
Romsey Road, Maybush, Southampton
SO9 4DH. Tel: 0703 792764/5 or 792749

Ordnance Survey maps of the North York Moors

The North York Moors area is covered by Ordnance Survey 1:50 000 scale (1¼ inches to 1 mile) Landranger map sheets 93, 94, 100 and 101. These all-purpose maps are packed with information to help you explore the area. Viewpoints, picnic sites, places of interest, caravan and camping sites are shown, as well as public rights of way information such as footpaths and bridle-ways.

To examine the North York Moors in more detail and especially if you are planning walks, Ordnance Survey Outdoor Leisure maps at 1:25 000 scale (2½ inches to 1 mile) are ideal.

Two such maps cover the area:

Sheet 26 — North York Moors
              Western area
Sheet 27 — North York Moors
              Eastern area

Areas not available in the Outdoor Leisure map series are instead covered by Pathfinder maps. Also at 1:25 000 scale (2½ inches to 1 mile), these are the perfect maps for walkers.

To look at the area surrounding the North York Moors, Ordnance Survey Routemaster maps at 1:250 000 scale (1 inch to 4 miles) will prove most useful. Sheet 5 (Northern England) and Sheet 6 (East Midlands and Yorkshire) are relevant.

Ordnance Survey maps and guides are available from most booksellers, stationers and newsagents.

Index